No Money, No Stuff

A probabilistic guide on building wealth

Jordan Du Bois

Copyright © 2020 Jordan Du Bois

All rights reserved.

ISBN: No ISBN here. Didn't want to waste $125 on this shit...

DEDICATION

I used a 6 x 9 template for the correct formatting of this book, so here's to you template. Thanks for making my life so much easier.

Image 1: Me.

Preface

On the surface, this book is about money, but my motivation for writing it is a disgust for the charlatans of the financial sector underbelly, or who I like to refer to as "SCAM SCUM;" the uneducated, slimy snake oil salesmen and the abundance of "gurus" on YouTube and other forums giving misguided, and sometimes downright dangerous advice. The very basics of becoming wealthy are all you need to hear to get started on the right path. The core tenets have not evolved over time - they are: determination, work ethic, logic, and an understanding of things which historically make money. The latter are referred to as wealth generating assets in this book, but they are no more than my educated guess based on my experiences and historical data when available. Wealth is a game of probability, and so, luck plays a role; increasing the probability of you becoming lucky, and therefore wealthy, is my goal with this book. I employ an approach that is known as abductive reasoning, which basically means I am guessing to my best ability. This book does not offer some bullshit pipe dream that investing in stocks, house hacking, or any of the other more esoteric strategies will make you wealthy on their own; investing in these things is a small piece of the wealth generating asset pie. I am extremely skeptical of anyone claiming to have made their millions through investing in stocks, real estate or some other financial asset alone and you should be as well, especially when they are trying to sell you their "system for success."

There are people, of course, who have made their money through investing in stocks or real estate, but for the vast majority, investing in such things will not lead to wealth in the short term - it will most likely not lead to wealth in the long term either, if that is all you pursue while being less than a millionaire. The risks and uncertainties more often than not eat people's money away who do not invest for the long term, or do not perform the necessary research prior to purchasing investments. Before educating myself in risk and financial assets, I lost money investing short term in both stocks and options, my friends have lost money investing, my father has lost money investing, and many others that I have encountered while being involved in real estate have lost everything trying to become a landlord or flipping houses. These are not dummies, but people who are at least college educated and have a technical career. I have been to seminars with friends and family and have heard and seen firsthand the SCAM SCUM giving an emotionally charged anecdote, often involving children, about how the system they are sharing led to their financial freedom. I have seen desperate hurting people in need put all of their savings towards one of these egregious marketing pyramid schemes. This book is like a vaccine to those types of scams and incorrect information. Where I am terse, I have provided links to external supplemental reading which can serve to foster a deeper understanding than what is given in this book. This book is an overview, but I try to elaborate on the information I believe is the most important for a strong financial foundation - the core tenets. This book is not for those who are already wealthy and will most likely stay that way due to their prudence and financial wisdom, or those looking for more than the basic tax loopholes, deductions and credits. This book is for those in need of a solid foundation in money management and financial opportunity. If there are words you don't understand, read this book with a dictionary app by your side. There are not many pages in this book, but please don't try and speed read it. Understanding the material is far more important.

Here's to your financial and mental health.

CONTENTS

1	My Background	1
2	Budget Basics	7
3	Increase Value, Increase Pay	17
4	Taxes	23
5	More Money Math	34
6	Minimalism	51
7	A Wealth of Mindsets	55
8	Road to Wealth	57
9	Appendix	60
10	About the Author	64

My Background

My family has had many characters with various job titles. There was the distributor, the chef, the acquisition expert, and then there was my dad, the blue collar man. These characters are not what you might be thinking; they did not work in the job that convention would ascribe to their titles. The distributor was great at being a salesman, even though what was distributed really needed no sales pitch - all it needed were fiends. The hottest items were cocaine, marijuana, and methamphetamine. The latter dominated the monthly sales numbers; its month over month sales graph would put a smile on any CEO's face. The chef was great at one thing, cooking meth. He was also good at fixing watches, but that didn't bring him much profit. Being a full-time cook was tiring, lonely, and very dangerous - he had to cook in a cave in the hills of California so the aromatic gases released during chemical reactions wouldn't land him in prison, or blow up the neighborhood. The cash it brought in was as addicting as the substance, so the cook pursued it up until someone killed him. Drug sale and manufacturing wasn't everybody's thing; there was also burglary. The acquisition expert, as his title suggests, was able to acquire almost anything. He would simply go into anyone's house with a shotgun and take whatever he wanted. This was a time before homes had WiFi cameras and alarms, making it relatively easy to be a thief. Yep, I come from a family of outlaws bent on doing whatever it took to make fast cash, chasing the fantasy of lavish living. I'm confident in saying they didn't achieve what they wanted: sons and daughters growing up without a mommy and daddy, drug and gambling addictions, pain during moments of sobriety, and death. They were too caught up in the chase.

My dad grew up around all of this chaos and wanted nothing to do with it. He wanted to earn a living the way he thought was right. He watched his mother work countless hours at the local hospital as a nurse which yielded enough money to feed a household of 8, as well as help fund college for one of the members. This work ethic was instilled in my father at a young age, and mixed with his entrepreneurial desires, became what he needed to start his own T-shirt selling business in his teens; it didn't make him a millionaire, but it was great side hustle income in addition to his manual labor day jobs. If my father would've been able to read this book, or any other guide on growing wealth, he may have been able to propel himself and our family into financial success even before he had his first kid, me. But that wasn't the case (if it were, we'd be in a Marty McFly situation), and most of his money was quickly spent on having fun as a teen, who until now, was forced to live on an extreme budget set forth by his mother, or starve. He worked day and night to make money and had no one in his corner telling him how fast the future would come, or that money could make more money. He was doing well for himself at age 17, but unfortunately the previously mentioned characters we're so tangled up with his life that he had to leave the state to find a safe place to live, saying goodbye to his income.

My father was tenacious though and didn't let anything stop him. He was extremely athletic and heard that boxing could pay handsomely, so he began training for his first fight. After multiple wins and earning the Golden Gloves title, he had what looked like a promising career. Then, I came along, and the thought of becoming punch drunk was too strong to bear so he left his boxing dreams to work in construction for some podunk outfit. The work was tough but the pay was semi-decent, especially for someone with no college and little high school. Unfortunately the amount of hours per week didn't bring in enough to sustain his new wife and kid. He would visit beaches in the evening after work and pick up cans and aluminum scrap for recycling money. One night while picking up beer cans on Ventura Beach, he got the idea for his next business venture: Scrap Man, with the slogan "We'll pick up your broken spaceship." Some jobs gave him decent payouts, but didn't yield anything substantial. Bills quickly ate his earnings from both income sources, and again he found himself in poverty looking for another opportunity.

He had a friend from childhood move to Arizona and become a successful general contractor who oversaw commercial building projects, and as fate would have it, was in need of a good construction worker. My dad kept in touch with this friend over the years, so he knew my dad had construction experience and offered him the position. There was zero hesitation: my dad packed our van up with everything we owned, we made one stop at McDonald's for coffee and a big breakfast platter at about 4 AM, and continued to Arizona. Fast forward 20 years, my father had become a successful foreman making over $50,000 a year, and decided to create his own construction company, Paramount Masonry, in which he would fix every inefficiency he observed running jobs. I joined him, drew his company logo, and aspired to rule the world with this new money making machine. Well, not so fast. You see, his company was formed in 2006 and with still little financial acumen and a lack of a working crystal ball, the Great Recession of 2008 not only destroyed his business, but took our trucks, house and every last scaffold plank our family owned. The IRS was owed a hefty chunk of money for his million dollar earnings in 2007, which may or may not have been able to be fought due to the loss of everything else, and he simply didn't have it, pouring every last cent into trying to keep his business alive. Nevertheless, like an indifferent mob boss, they cleaned out the pittance his bank account held multiple times over the following years. He picked himself back up, suppressed his ego and depression, and went back to work for a rival construction company. I on the other hand absolutely abhorred construction and looked for employment elsewhere.

During 2006 I basically dropped out of high school. I took the two week fast track to obtaining my degree from e-institute, a joke of a school all computer-based, in a room filled with an omen of poverty and future convicts. Thus, my curriculum vitae was quite bare. After the collapse of Paramount Masonry I was on food stamps and knew a friend who knew some people who knew how to make some money. I did some odd jobs here and there, enough to pay for a cell phone and give my dad $200 a month for rent, as well as pay for a membership at the YMCA across the street. You get special discounts on YMCA memberships when you're on food stamps, which was how I could afford the monthly fee. After working out there for a couple months, I found out you can get a free membership as an employee, so I became an employee. The odd jobs were infrequent and the income amount from them undependable, so the YMCA was a good change. I now had a stable income, cut my membership bill, and was making enough to set aside money in a savings account. I didn't know much about building wealth, but I was blessed with decent impulse control and executive functioning, so I was able to save $5,000 after a year at the YMCA and buy a car cash. I had zero debt, other than recurring cell, rent, and car related bills, was making a steady income, and had prospects of becoming a personal trainer which would boost my income from $7.50 an hour to a base salary of $13 an hour.

The fantasies and visions of me becoming wealthy and ruling the world suddenly began to reappear in my mind. I should have learned from going through the 2008 crisis that nothing is set in stone when it comes to finances, and so wouldn't have had my hopes and dreams shattered when the YMCA suddenly shifted management and made it mandatory to have a bachelor's degree in exercise science to become a personal trainer. I put in hours of time going to class after class through the YMCA Trainer program which ended up being unusable due to the management change. Frustrated, I left my low scum paying position without giving my two weeks notice and moved up in the world to slinging lattes at Starbucks for $7.75 an hour. This was quite an interesting job which gave me much insight into the world of the wealthy. Prior to this, I never knowingly conversed with anyone who was wealthy. My first day on the job was at one of the busiest locations in Arizona, Desert Ridge, a section of area between Phoenix and Scottsdale; not close enough to obtain a coveted Scottsdale ZIP Code, but it did obtain many of its nasty inhabitants. They were fiendishly impatient; it was like dealing with crackheads. Then I moved up to the big time, becoming a shift supervisor and switching to another extremely busy location at the corner of Hayden Road and Thompson Peak. My pay went from $7.75 an hour to $8.15 an hour; I was practically rich.

This location was a Mecca for maniacs with extreme wealth, God complexes, and those desperately trying to stay with the in crowd, even though their finances were always teetering on the brink of extinction and their assets all owned by banks. I was privy to this knowledge from one of my coworkers, who according to her, was just there to pass the time and collect the sweet insurance benefits. She lived in DC Ranch, an opulent subdivision which my dad and I frequently took walks in, albeit as uninvited guests. As each person would come and go, often complaining about the level of foam that distinguished the latte from the cappuccino, she would come over to me and say, "oh that's so and so, his wife has a spending addiction and they're doing everything they can to maintain an air of status. They're about to go bankrupt and lose their house to foreclosure." I heard many of these stories from my nosy insider, but wanted to know how the money was made in the first place, so I remembered the customers she pointed out as very wealthy *and* stable. There was one old guy who drove a gold Aston Martin and owned a chain of hotels and restaurants in New York. I'd love to say he gave me some amazing insight that transformed my world and catapulted me to where I am today, but he was just a creepy old guy who loved to talk about the young girls he would hire at his restaurants and hotels. Then there was another old guy - most of the wealthy clientele were old by the way - who told me about how he was making a hefty income from his stock portfolio dividends, specifically AT&T, which did get me thinking about the meaning of passive income. Throughout the day assholes would come in complaining about insignificant things here and there; the fact that I was 30 seconds too late on their toaster pastry and now they're late for a work meeting, or some other bullshit that these rich pricks loved to blame on the poor, helpless baristas. I learned that the wealthy can be just like the poor, that their spending is similar, their drug addictions are similar, and they're assholes. The only thing that seemed to separate them was their knowledge of money acquisition. I further noted that what separated the wealthy from the soon to be bankrupt was the handling of their money in terms of investments, long term budgeting, and their psychology.

It was Thursday and I had the day off. I was looking in a magazine at a gun ad - I like guns - and by chance, came across an advertisement for Glendale Community College. The ad stated that there was financial help for anyone looking to attend and change their life. I knew nothing about college, nor did I ever think I would go, but when I went to the local library and searched online for financial incentives for college, I found that you could obtain what at the time was so much money to me, I immediately drove to the campus for a placement test. Due to my lack of education I was placed in the lowest level classes in all subjects, and due to my lack of money, was eligible for every grant and loan available. Each semester would yield a certain amount of money in grants and loans. I said goodbye to my Starbucks compadres, used the grants to pay for college and bills, and took all of the loan money and put it into AT&T stock like my wealthy old friend. College at this point was just a way for me to get more money into my hands than Starbucks, or any other job I was qualified on paper for could. I took some courses in math, science, and a bullshit course on the art of storytelling so that I would have a full schedule and qualify for the highest amount of money. I also had access to their newly remodeled gym, all covered by tuition.

Exercise got me thinking about biology and how the body is able to build muscle from this strange creature habit of picking things up that are heavy. I wanted to know more, so I looked up information on the Internet about building muscle and decided to bias my courses towards science. I started paying attention in class and became infatuated with learning. I didn't know the hierarchy of degrees and believed the 2 year degree I was obtaining there was all that was required for me to land a high paying job. I was in for a surprise when I spoke to an advisor who told me a two year degree is called an associates degree and it's practically worthless, other than obtaining prerequisites for a higher level degree such as a Bachelors, Masters, or Doctorate. Additionally, I would have to leave the community college and apply to get into a university to continue my education above the associates degree level. Eventually, my motivation and interest in learning about the human body, as well as mathematics, became so strong that I didn't really mind how long I had to be in school. I loved listening to good professors lecture, I could exercise, and I had access to all of their campus resources; I was in heaven.

Let's take a moment now and analyze my situation. I had a place to learn and hang out all day, a gym, food stamps, a paid off car, and money in a stock market account. At first glance some might think that my net worth included $5,000 for the car and $14,500 in the stock account, but this isn't the correct way, in my opinion, to categorize assets. The reason being anything you purchase which doesn't continue to make you money or appreciate in value should be considered a decreasing asset. The car would experience a certain level of depreciation every year, as well as require maintenance. Additionally, out of my $14,500 in the stock market, only $500 was my money and the rest was loan money that I would eventually have to pay back, making my net worth $5,500 if I sold the car for $5,000. I was bringing in an income from tutoring just enough to cover my bills and had no savings account, other than the stock account. Since I borrowed all required textbooks from the library and fellow students, I removed the need to purchase them, allowing more grant money to enter the stock account. I didn't know this was a bad financial move, and the stocks dropped, decreasing my account to $13,700. The old guy from Starbucks left out the part about risk, and since I thought investing was a sure thing, I didn't perform much due diligence before obtaining a brokerage account to invest.

With no emergency fund and only liability insurance, life quickly threw me another curveball. A woman high on drugs ran a red light and smashed into me, totaling my car. She had no insurance, and since I had liability only, my car sat in my backyard as scrap metal for about a year, until I could save up $700 to fix it. I didn't want to dip into the loan money in the stock market, as I was already technically in debt $300 from the loss of stock value. After a mechanic "fixed" the car, it broke down a few weeks later. Feeling robbed by the mechanic, I told him to repair it again for free, to which he said no, so I blew his house up. Just kidding, I salvaged my car for $500 and said goodbye to driving a car. I bought my next door neighbor's bike for $25 - who undoubtedly sold it cheap so he could get high on meth that day - and began saving $200 a month that was previously spent on gas and insurance. It turned out for the better, but illustrates the importance of thinking about material objects such as a car, as separate from net worth, unless it makes money, or retains monetary value. If you think about the reasons you want money and carefully list them in two categories: wants and needs, one will be a list of expenses, such as bills and food, that cannot be changed (if they could, you should always decrease them), and the other will be a list of things which can wait until you have wealth to purchase, or not. And now, let's add a third List with the category heading of Wealth Generating Assets, which we will discuss more throughout this book.

When building wealth, luck plays a role that many who experience it do not attribute enough credit; we've all heard of the person who made millions overnight in the stock market, or the genius who invented some high tech automated system and again made millions overnight. What do all of these events have in common, though? Well for one, they are all events, and if we look at it as such we can start thinking mathematically about wealth. In this book I'm not going to lay out get-rich-quick schemes of money generation, instead I am going to focus on a method of event grouping through experience and exposure to various subjects, as well as the psychology useful to building wealth. This is not a guaranteed strategy to financial success, but a probabilistic model which, like all models, is subject to various outcomes, not necessarily the one that you had hoped for. I still believe it's a superior way to try and obtain wealth through this style of thinking and doing, and therefore have written this book. I will keep what follows as concise as possible, while trying to make it an enjoyable read.

Budget Basics

No matter what level of income you make, you will never become wealthy spending most or all of it. One day you may get hit with an unforeseen expense, get injured, or have COVID-19 ruin your family business that has been operating for years. History should be a great teacher, but it seems people have a short memory when it comes to economic disasters. If you have nothing saved for situations like this, you will be looking at financial turmoil. The best plan of action is a budget. You need to create a money plan that takes into account all of your income and breaks it into categories which should be strictly adhered to. Recall the three lists from Chapter 1: Needs, Wants, and Wealth Generating Assets. We can subdivide these lists into subcategories:

- **Needs:**
  - **Fixed Expenses** : Car payment, insurance, rent/mortgage, phone, HOA
  - **Variable Expenses**: Food, gas, utilities,
  - **Emergency Fund:** Should be enough to cover all of your recurring expenses (fixed and variable) for one year. This is built up over time using a percentage approach.
  - **Retirement Fund**: There may be a time when you don't want to/ are unable to work, and social security may not be there.
- **Wants:**
  - **Entertainment and Restaurants**: Going out to eat, Starbucks, Netflix subscription.
  - **Savings Fund**: New clothes, New car, New house, Vacation, etc...
- **Wealth Generating Assets (Investments/Gambles):**
  - **Education**: College or Trade School, Audible, Books, MOOCS.
  - **Financial Instruments**: Treasury Bills, Bonds, CDs, Stocks, Index Funds, Real Property, etc...
  - **Business Venture Capital:** If you aspire to create your own business, you need some amount of start up funds, even for a business with low overhead.

➢ **High-yield Savings Account:** If you want a place to store your wealth without much investment risk, look into a savings account that pays you to keep it there.

We now see some possible categories to allocate our income. The budget is created by assigning a percentage to each category such that any income is automatically partitioned appropriately. The ideal budget should potentially lead to an accumulation of wealth, so we need to assign percentages that will allow for this. We must also remember to use after tax income so that we don't budget money we don't have. I recommend figuring out which tax bracket you fall into so that you can subtract that percentage from your income to get your net income, or take home pay, and any write-offs and tax credits you have which reduces this amount will be bonus income; we will discuss taxes in more detail in chapter 4. For now, we will be using SmartAsset's tax estimate calculator. Math works better with an example, so consider the following scenarios with a seven category budget:

Scenario 1:

Jack's income totals $12,000 per year, which is less than the poverty level set by the US government. Each month Jack brings in $1,000 from doing handyman work, and so he falls under independent contractor for tax purposes. His taxes are brutal and look like this:

Federal: $0
FICA (self-employed rate of 15.3%): $1,836
State (assuming IL): $481
Total: **$2,317** (19.3% of income)

Jack's net income is gross income minus income taxes above, so $12,000 - $2,317 = $9,683 divided by 12 months is approximately $807 per month which will be budgeted as follows:

Fixed Expenses (35%) = $282.45
Variable Expenses (20%) = $161.40
Emergency Fund (20%) = $161.40
Retirement Fund (10%) = $80.70
Entertainment (0%) = $0
Savings Fund (5%) = $40.35
All Investments Fund (10%) = $80.70

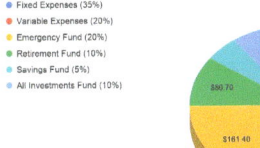
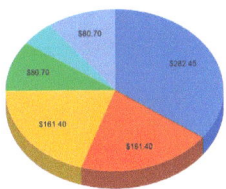

As you can see from this example, Jack has very little to work with, but he can apply for government assistance to help with the cost of food, housing, and medical, as well as education using grants. Jack can also qualify for IRS credits such as the Earned Income Tax Credit and Savers Credit. At the end of the year, Jack will have $484 in savings, $1,936 in emergency, $968 in retirement, and $968 in investments. You can see even poverty level income with these percentages can accumulate money. This budget reduces the chance of Jack going into debt, and while this will not make Jack wealthy by any stretch of the imagination, it is a great start.

Scenario 2:

Jill has a gross income of $28,800 putting her around the 35th percentile which just means this is still a relatively low income for a US citizen. Her monthly pay is $2,400 as a W2 employee for tax purposes. As an employee, Jill has less freedom with write-offs when compared to an independent contractor, but she still has the Federal standard deduction of $12,200 (2019 rate), IL State deduction of $2275, and the Earned Income Tax Credit of $538 (IRS Website). We will use the SmartAsset calculator to determine her Federal, FICA, and State Taxes, ignoring any credits and just considering the standard deductions:

Federal: $1,798
FICA(employee rate of 7.65%): $2,203
State (assuming IL): $1,313
Total: **$5,314** (18.45% of income)

And so, her monthly net income is $28,800 - $5,314 = $23,486 divided by 12 months is $1,957 per month which will be budgeted as follows:

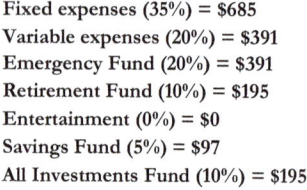
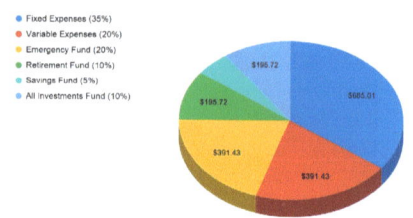

Fixed expenses (35%) = $685
Variable expenses (20%) = $391
Emergency Fund (20%) = $391
Retirement Fund (10%) = $195
Entertainment (0%) = $0
Savings Fund (5%) = $97
All Investments Fund (10%) = $195

Jill's allocation is looking pretty decent. She doesn't qualify for food stamps, but she does qualify for College Financial Aid (Government Help).

These scenarios assume the ability of each person to stick to a budget because it assumes their bills will be covered by their allocation to the expense categories, but let's be real, ALMOST NOBODY can live a decent life on a poverty level income, let alone become wealthy if they are on their own with no help from relatives. In fact, working full time for the current federal minimum wage of $7.25 per hour (Department of Labor) will yield an income of $13,920, and poverty level is just a tad below that at $12,760. According to the Economic Policy Institute, it takes approximately $2,500 per month in one of the most affordable US cities - Sunflower County, Mississippi - for an individual with no children to pay for a life that will support proper nutrition, housing and insurance. Jack and Jill don't get anywhere near this! Even if one did have help and was able to abide by Jack's budget combining savings, retirement, and investment allocations into a ROTH IRA (to avoid taxes on earnings, see Chapter 4) which would equal $2,421 a year, and looking at a fantasy scenario of 10% return compounded annually year over year - we'll see in Chapter 5 why this may be difficult/impossible to obtain - you would have approximately $3,102,025.80 after 50 years. If we assume inflation will be 3% per year, we have an inflation adjusted return (what is known as a real return) of $858,090, which just means that your $3.1 million will have as much purchasing power as $858,090 currently does (inflation adjusted investment calculator). Pretty shitty right? Another unfortunate fact is most people from low income families have kids before they have a career, tons of credit card and loan debt, and zero time because they work multiple jobs. I get it. The struggle is real! What can be done for people in this situation? Sell your organs - but seriously - the first thing is to spend less, if possible, so ANY kind of budget that allows you to do this will be beneficial. If you are in debt you need to ask yourself what created the debt - was it bills such as renting a modest place to live, or did buying unnecessary shit like an Apple watch do it? If the latter, sell your shit, pay your bills, and learn from your dumbass mistakes. There are only so many things that you can do when you are strapped for cash, can barely pay your bills, and have no one to help you. Just do what you have to do to survive, always be looking for the highest pay you can get at your current job or elsewhere, and create a budget asap.

Let's consider one more scenario, as not everyone is living on poverty level pay. According to statistics from Census.gov, the median income in 2018 was $61,937 so let's use that number. Note also that I am using the median as a measure of income because it is the number that 50% of the population falls below and 50% are above, so in terms of probability, picking an employee at random from the US yields a 50% chance that they are at or above this income.

Scenario 3:

Mary makes the 2018 median income of $61,937 which puts her at approximately $5,161 per month. We will assume she is a regular W2 employee and has only the standard deduction. We will use the same calculator from SmartAsset as we used with Jack and Jill to determine her Federal, FICA, and State Taxes:

Federal: $6,801
FICA(employee rate of 7.65%): $4,738
State (assuming IL): $2,953
Total: $14,492 (23.40% of income)

Her budget will be based on an after tax amount of $47,445, which breaks down to $3,953.75 per month:

Recurring Fixed Expenses (35%) = $1,383
Recurring Variable Expenses (20%) = $790
Emergency Fund (20%) = $790
Retirement Fund (10%) = $395
Entertainment (0%) = $0
Savings Fund (5%) = $197
All Investments Fund (10%) = $395

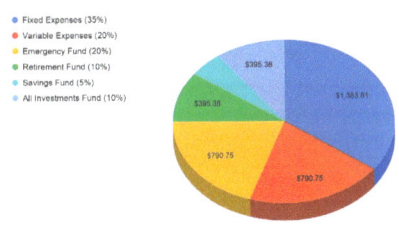

I have been using 0% for entertainment because I don't think money should be spent on it when trying to save and change your life, but when you reach the median income, maybe you will want to change it to accommodate subscriptions to services such as Amazon, Netflix, or Audible, and treat yourself to the occasional Cafe Mocha. From Mary's budget we can see that she will have $9,489 in her Emergency Fund, $4,744 in her retirement account, $2,372 in her savings, and $4,744 in her investment account at the end of each year. Here are two summary tables showing the monthly budget, as well as the yearly budget for all 3 scenarios.

Monthly Budget Summary	Scenario 1	Scenario 2	Scenario 3
After Tax Income	$807.00	$1,957.17	$3,953.75
Recurring fixed expenses (35%) = $783	$282.45	$685.01	$1,383.81
Recurring variable expenses (20%) = $447	$161.40	$391.43	$790.75
Emergency Fund (20%) = $447	$161.40	$391.43	$790.75
Retirement Fund (10%) = $224	$80.70	$195.72	$395.38
Entertainment (0%) = $0	$0.00	$0.00	$0.00
Savings Fund (5%) = $112	$40.35	$97.86	$197.69
All Investments Fund (10%) = $224	$80.70	$195.72	$395.38

Table 1: Monthly summary budget for each scenario. Light red are expenses.

Yearly Budget Summary	Scenario 1	Scenario 2	Scenario 3
After Tax Income	$9,684.00	$23,486.00	$47,445.00
Recurring fixed expenses (35%)	$3,389.40	$8,220.10	$16,605.75
Recurring variable expenses (20%)	$1,936.80	$4,697.20	$9,489.00
Emergency Fund (20%)	$1,936.80	$4,697.20	$9,489.00
Retirement Fund (10%)	$968.40	$2,348.60	$4,744.50
Entertainment (0%)	$0.00	$0.00	$0.00
Savings Fund (5%)	$484.20	$1,174.30	$2,372.25
All Investments Fund	$968.40	$2,348.60	$4,744.50
50 yr investment return (10% compounded)	$1,240,810.32	$3,009,259.73	$6,079,124.92

Table 2: Yearly summary budget for each scenario. Light red are expenses.

Creating the budget can be as easy as writing it down on a napkin and sticking to it with every paycheck that comes in. I'm fancy, so a napkin simply doesn't cut it. I like to use Google Sheets because of its formulas and ability to be programmed using Google App Scripts, which opens up the ability to bring in data from other sources, such as tax and investment data, so that was my first go-to. To see the spreadsheet budget I constructed, CLICK HERE. You can also copy the sheet to your Google Drive by clicking on File → Make a copy and change it to suit you. Just know that the tax section is broken because I abandoned it after I came to the conclusion that I do not want to update the formulas each time the tax brackets change. I now simply rely on a site which is constantly updating them, like SmartAsset.com, to calculate my taxes, then I create my after-tax budget accordingly. Even though this spreadsheet is old news, it can still help you see how formulas are used in Google Sheets, and you can still create a budget. Learning how to use Google Sheets and its associated programs, such as App Scripts, is a great skill to have. Knowledge of Google Sheets will also be beneficial when we discuss some advanced investing topics and look at creating simulations for portfolio optimization in Chapter 5. Don't worry if this is over your head, you can still accumulate wealth with the simple advice in this book. I've basically included Chapter 5 for those wishing to see a little more deeply into the math of finance, and I'm a math fanatic, so I wanted to.

If you don't want to create your own budget app from scratch - or if you are denied api (application programming interface, used to obtain bank account data programmatically) access from your bank like I was, leaving you cold and confused - another tech option that can be very beneficial is an app on your phone. I use Intuit's Quickbooks for my businesses, and was thrilled to discover they have a web and phone app called MINT. You have the ability to link up your checking and savings accounts, as well as your bills, which MINT will send you reminders about before they are due. To stick to a budget, this is key; you can't have your budget just sitting in a spreadsheet disconnected from your spending. When I was turned down for a bank api, this was the reality; if I wanted to stick to my Google Sheet budget, I would have to manually track every single bank account, writing down all expenses, and comparing it to my budget to see if I was sticking to it. MINT tracks all of the activity on the accounts you hook up to it, even credit cards, so I let out a big HECK YES when I read through what MINT had to offer. Side note: If you are *extremely* careful you can use credit cards for their rewards, but only if you pay them off before they are due, and ONLY if you have the money to make the purchase without the credit card. If you need help building a great credit score, get the [Credit Karma app](#) and follow their guidelines, it's as simple as that.

One last word on budgeting, it can be helpful if you have one account for all of your expenses to be paid from - I use credit cards to pay certain expenses so that I earn rewards, but they are set up on auto-pay with my designated expense checking account - and other interest earning accounts to hold your non-expense money such as savings, investment, and retirement money. At the time of writing this book, I use [Wealthfront's](#) high yield savings (which is not currently so high yield) and their robo investing platform for a portion of my investment money. Strategic placement and usage of your money can aid in building wealth when you have a good amount coming in each month, as well as good credit so you can obtain the cash back credit cards, and low interest loans if you absolutely must borrow money. When I say this can aid in building wealth, I am referring to this type of mindset more so than the amount of money it brings in. More often than not, people get lost in the forest when they are looking too intensely at each tree's detail. For example, trying to mass wealth through credit card hacking - a term used to describe "optimal" use of credit cards by exploiting card sign on bonuses and attempting to obtain max points and rewards - can be extremely tedious, dizzying, and lead to negative consequences buried in each credit card's terms and conditions. In my opinion, it often doesn't make sense for the average person to focus on these sorts of parlor tricks. Once you have the basic covered: high paying job, low monthly spending, and a stellar budget track record, then *perhaps* you can play around with those kinds of things, but don't go out of your way chasing this little bullshit stuff.

Monthly CC Expenses	$1,087.28
Monthly CC Rewards	$21.75
Monthly Account Interest	$27.68
Total Cash Earned (Yearly)	$593.06

Table 3: Example of money earned with a 2% cash back rewards credit card that is used to pay half of the monthly expenses, and a 2% annual return on combined savings, emergency, and investment accounts totalling $16,605.75 as of January in that year.

Budget Category	**Good Account Types**
Savings	High Yield Savings, Money Market
Emergency	High Yield Savings, Money Market,
Retirement	IRA, 401(K), High Yield Savings
Expenses	High Yield Checking
Investments	High Yield Savings, Money Market

Table 4: Account types to choose for optimal interest AND appropriate liquidity prior to using the funds. You should NEVER put money that you need in less than 10 years into a high risk account, such as the stock market, as it could lose money quickly.

What is An IRA, Anyway?

Looking at Table 4 you may see account types that you have never heard of before, or have heard of but know nothing about such as an IRA, 401(K) or Money Market, so I want to discuss the basics of them here. Let's start with the IRA, which simply stands for Individual Retirement Account. The IRA, as the name implies, is a form of retirement account and it comes in a few different flavors such as Traditional, Roth, and SIMPLE; there are others, but these are generally regarded as the most well-known. These IRA distinctions have their pros and cons - and it is best to look at each one with a professional if you don't have the time to research the terms and conditions yourself - but they are nothing more than an account to hold investments in; they are not investments on their own. The type of IRA chosen dictates which investments can be put into them, and are usually restricted to the investments offered by the bank/financial institution you set them up with. There is also a Self-directed IRA which allows you the most freedom when choosing investments; things like real estate, tax liens, and precious metals are often available through the institutions which offer Self-directed IRAs (see THIS LIST for more info). The 401(k) is another type of retirement account which is offered by some employers for their employees; this is really the main difference between an IRA and 401(k). You can have multiple retirement accounts, but the contribution limits for each type apply cumulatively, so if you have three ROTH IRAs your contribution limit for the sum of all three is still the same as contributing to just one, and in 2020 that amount is $6,000 if you are under 50 years of age. To learn more about retirement accounts, check out this IRS PAGE. The other types of accounts mentioned - High Yield Savings/Checking, Money Market (not the Mutual Fund) - are all considered low risk accounts that are usually suitable for storage of money short-term, or long term if you hate the idea of investing, and have rates of return which fluctuate according to the Federal funds interest rate. For example, Wealthfront used to offer 2.50% annual return on their High Yield Savings account back in 2019 when the Federal funds target range was 2.25% - 2.50%. Here's my 0.02 cents: all of these accounts with their rules and fluctuating rates should be put into a database or simple spreadsheet, out of which a personalized plan of action could be created based on your current situation: employment status, marital status, and so forth… Oh wait, is that what SoFi did?

Increase Value, Increase Pay

The budget is mandatory to build wealth at any stage in life, but this is a probabilistic book and we want to stack the odds of becoming wealthy in our favor, so we need more. Specifically, we need to earn more per hour. I can hear it now, you are saying, "well, no shit Sherlock!" But don't worry, I'm not going to go over schemes here, or simply tell you to become a neurosurgeon and you're all good. Instead, I want to guide you to finding answers to questions regarding high-paying career paths, financing the required education, and resources to beef up your chances of landing a killer job. In America, unique ability is proportional to pay; the more unique your skills, the higher your pay, generally speaking. Getting a degree alone is not enough to land a job in this competitive world. You need to stand out from the other candidates by completing internships, having practical experience, and networking, in addition to a degree. If you want to own your own business, going to college definitely won't hurt. I own multiple businesses, but before I was even remotely successful, I was in college for six years earning two degrees and had lost money on other business startups. You need options - remember, our approach is to stack odds in our favor. Who is most likely to become rich, based on current stats, the person who has a dream of owning their own business and a few bucks to throw at it, or the person who has that in addition to a degree, experience, and a network of colleagues?

Financing College

First, you must know that I am against having debt, if possible. I would rather have less things and forego the pursuit of investments that can lead me to financial ruin, than try to leverage debt on a risky investment. College is no exception. There are degrees that historically lead to careers which pay lots of money, and there are degrees that don't. I would not feel comfortable obtaining debt to fund the degrees which do not usually lead to high paying careers, and we will see in the next section how to avoid choosing such degrees. This does not guarantee that we will make lots of money, as it is all historical data, and a shifting economy tends to erase careers which used to be thought of as safe bets. In our current economy of 2020, automation is highly disrupting the medical industry, financial industry, and many other high-paying fields, but it is helpful to know the trends of what usually pays and what doesn't to make a better guess. With the current uncertainty of the future economy, extra caution must be maintained to get through college with as little debt as possible. If you are in high school, great, you can start early on by trying to obtain scholarships with good grades and extracurricular activities. If you are like me, meaning you pissed your scholarship opportunities off because you hated school and everyone in your classes, you will have to look for financing for college and possibly start from the bottom in entry-level courses. Not a problem, I got you! To see how much you can qualify for, you need to visit studentaid.gov and fill out the Free Application for Federal Student Aid (FAFSA). I was poor as dirt when I applied so my entire first Bachelor's degree and most of my second Bachelor's degree were completely paid for. I started at Glendale Community College, as I mentioned earlier, and then went to Arizona State University - practically all for free. This is an important step because community colleges are usually much more affordable than universities, and since many people attend college and fail, making mistakes at the community college level is much less costly. Additionally, you can apply for a job on campus: one avenue is the work study program. Bonus tip, apply to become a tutor in the subjects you are learning, that way you will solidify concepts that you will need in upper level courses, as well as make money. Win-Win.

There are multiple methods of funding education, some of which need to be paid back such as federal loans. You want the grants and scholarships initially because you don't need to pay them back, so after you apply for the FAFSA, look at this page on the same website: FAFSA - Scholarships These applications are ABSOLUTELY FREE, and that webpage points out the fact there are scams out there that ask you for money. Just stick with what studentaid.gov tells you to do and you may be getting that lovely free cheddar in no time! Lastly, check out the loans. This is an area in which you need extreme caution and discipline in order to benefit, but it is possible to benefit. Each year you will be offered a type of loan known as a subsidized loan which does not start accruing interest until you graduate or reduce your full-time status. This is the key to getting money from these loans, as they can be placed in a practically risk-free option to earn interest such as a treasury bill, CD, or high yield savings account. At the time of writing this book (March 2020) rates are dismal, hovering around 1% return for a CD, so you may want to skip the loans all together if earning $10 for every thousand dollars locked up each year sounds pointless to you. I advise against playing with loan money in the stock market like I did. Yes, you may be able to make money, but the risk in my opinion is not worth it (see Chapter 5 for a discussion on risk to learn more).

Lasty, if you are a parent trying to save money for your children's education, you may hear about the college [529 Plan](), which is known as a qualified tuition plan, and covers certain costs associated with college such as [tuition, room and board, and textbooks](). The contribution limit is set per state, but if you contribute more than the current year's gift limit - $15,000 in 2020 - you will have to pay gift tax. Here is some more bad news: having this plan will affect the amount attainable through FAFSA, as the balance in the 529 account is a factor on the FAFSA application under Expected Family Contribution. Let's not forget that this plan can also lose money because you are investing the money in the stock market. I think it's much less risky to just have Uncle Sam foot as much of the bill as possible for your child's college; taxpayers pay into financial aid programs for this purpose, so why allow the Government to build up a reserve of unused tax dollars to spend on hookers?

Careers and Colleagues

Now that we know we can get funding for school, lets see how we can pick a couple of degrees to compare in terms of pay, current and future demand, and necessity for higher-level education beyond the four year bachelor's degree. I didn't include finding a career based on your passion because you may not know you had a passion for data analysis until you start. OH AND, AND, AND, do you really have a passion for a low paying job, lack of funds, or the inability to indulge in your passion due to ZERO time because you need multiple jobs? Of course not. There are two options to look at for accurate pay data connected to a college degree that I know about: [College Scorecard]() and [Post-Secondary Employment Outcomes]() (PSEO). I favor PSEO because College Scorecard uses data only from students who received financial aid, and thus biases the outcomes towards them. Additionally, College Scorecard does not allow you to see which fields the graduates are working in, and that is a very important factor in answering the question of which degree to choose. The tool at PSEO allows us to see the amount of money being earned by graduates with bachelor's degrees (and higher), how long after graduation it took to reach a certain salary, as well as if they are working in their field of study or not. After playing with the PSEO tool, take note of a couple career paths and check them out at Salary.com and Google for Jobs to see what recruiters are looking for in terms of experience. You can use this information to apply to the right internships early on in college. This all happens before we sign up for our first college course so that we don't waste money - the federal funds do run out - and time. Here is a video for your reference: Exploring Career Paths with PSEO

College is not just about learning, it's also about networking. Don't overlook networking because you may graduate and not be able to find a job, but your colleagues may, and can then put in a good word for you. There are also many opportunities to land great internships through your professors, so get to know them as well. When I was going through college, I had zero knowledge that this was what I should have been doing, and so had zero internship experience when I graduated. I have many colleagues who became friends with the professors, were given internship and research program opportunities, and ended up taking a job at one of the companies they interned with. I'm not talking garbage companies either: Google, Intel, Microsoft, and Banner Health to name a few. Many times landing a job is about who you know; this is a great example of this book's recurring theme: stacking the odds of wealth in your favor. Don't sit around hugging your degree(s), rocking back and forth while frantically monitoring your email inbox for messages from job recruiting sites. Just make that network of friends, take intern opportunities, and that will help tremendously.

MOOCS

If you want to increase your knowledge on a specific topic to help you ascend the company ladder at your current employer, you can also check out Massive Online Open Courses, or MOOCS for short. These are full courses on topics ranging from understanding obesity to database management and many more. I personally use Coursera to improve my technical knowledge of programming with their courses and their Guided Projects, but there are many other MOOCS out there. Coursera is free to audit any course, meaning you can go through all of the material for free, but will not get a certificate of completion at the end, and the courses are taught by some of the best professors in the industry. Now, I don't know anyone personally who has obtained a MOOC certificate and landed a high paying job because of it, but learning new skills is always beneficial, and you can add it to your resume or curriculum vitae (sounds so fancy). I have not paid for one MOOC yet but have obtained knowledge from courses such as Learning How To Learn by Barbara Oakley, Python for Data Science, Machine Learning, Philosophy, and Logic. When I was regularly applying to jobs right out of college, I would put what I had learned through these courses on my job applications, as well as update my CV on LinkedIn, Indeed, and a few other job boards. I still receive calls and emails from hiring departments at software development companies and labs. It feels strange to turn down jobs with starting salaries of $65,000 because my businesses made me wealthy, but at least I have a backup if my companies go under and all my wealth generating assets disintegrate. Remember that the position you work now can be used as experience for a field you are wanting to enter, especially if you have education credentials, and double especially if you eloquently articulate your experience on your resume. Example: instead of typing your previous job description as "Subway Slave - made sandwiches cleaned toilets dealt with assholes all day," you could put: "Subway Meal Artisan - carefully crafted the perfect sandwich with a blend of cheeses, meats, vegetables and fresh baked breads, and offered relevant and tastefully appropriate suggestions for side dishes to improve the culinary experience of each Subway patron." I would definitely hire someone with that on their resume!

Retain What You Learn

Whether you attend College, enroll in MOOCs, or learn from YouTube, you need to keep the useful information in memory and be able to retrieve it when needed. I personally employ habits which are backed by what I consider high quality scientific studies, such as spaced repetition. I dive deeper into learning and ways to train your brain in my upcoming book How to Ascend Biology, so I will just refer you to that if you are interested, but wanted to briefly mention learning because you cannot offer value to an employer, or as an employer, if you don't retain the information which makes you valuable. One of the learning habits I have involves studying flashcards. You can download the flashcard software ANKI for free if you have an android, or $25 if you have an iPhone, or you can just use the free web based app which I use. What makes this program so useful is it's space repetition algorithm which is based on presenting you flashcards at specific time intervals thought to help you retain the information. Effects of this style of studying have been published by researchers such as Robert and Elizabeth Björk, who have coined the term desirable difficulties, simply meaning stuff that is tough on your brain but helps you retain (I'm gonna trademark that). This, in my opinion, is a great way to actually learn something when you're not immersed in it day to day, as you are with a job. If you are hoping to land a computer programming job for example, many companies ask you to pass a test before they will even consider interviewing you. There are even companies whose sole purpose is creating tests that are industry specific - check out this directory - which hiring departments are leveraging to find great candidates due to the ever increasing applicant pool with college degrees. Side note: I see the value of college degrees declining every year due to the supply of new grads, which is why it is more important than ever to consider the advice in this chapter. When I first started out in college I heard of people obtaining associates degrees - a 2 year degree - and landing great jobs; by the time I graduated, most bachelor's degrees were practically useless in obtaining a high-paying career and were only used as stepping stones to obtain some other higher education degree in order to make a yearly salary of $60,000 - $100,000. If you watch the post secondary employment outcomes video I linked to above you will see that there are not many career fields that will pay $100,000 yearly with only a bachelor's degree, even after 10 years at the company. I don't believe that the cost of the majority of degrees is warranted these days, which is why I am very happy that I received financial aid, and why I started the chapter out with how to obtain it.

Taxes

Disclaimer: I am not a certified public accountant, lawyer, or tax professional, so don't take this information in place of a recognized tax professional's advice; I just really care about my money, and so, have invested considerable time in trying to understand taxes and how to reduce them legally.

If you were to write down a list of all expenses which eat your money and reduce your purchasing power before you even think about spending it, then organize that list from highest to lowest, chances are the category of taxes would be at the top. Here are the tax categories that US citizens can be subject to:

☆☆☆ Types of Taxes in the US ☆☆☆			
☆ Tax ☆	☆ What it is ☆	☆ How Much ☆	☆ What it's spent on ☆
Federal Income	tax on ordinary income sources and short term capital gains, varies by income. (Ex: wages, certain dividends)	0-37% (marginal)	Military, National Debt, Bloated Politicians, Social Programs, Education
State Income	tax on ordinary income sources, varies by income and state.	0-9.53% (marginal)	Community infrastructure, Bloated Politicians, Social Programs, Education
Capital Gains	tax on long term capital gains (Ex: stocks, house sale)	0-20%	Same as Federal Income Tax
Payroll (FICA)	tax on ordinary income sources. Employer pays half, employee pays half	15.30%	Medicare, Medicaid, the Children's Health Insurance Program (CHIP), and Affordable Care Act (ACA) marketplace subsidies

Property	tax on assessed value of real estate, varies by state.	0-4%	State and local debt, Libraries and community, Bloated Politicians
State and Local Sales and Use	tax on consumed goods, varies by state.	0-9.53%	Same as State Income Tax
Estate	tax on passing valuables to heirs at death, varies by amount. Only applies to inheritances above $11 million as of 2020	18-40%	Same as Federal Income Tax
Gift	tax on gifts given, varies by situation.	0-40%	Government shit, Bloated Politicians, I'm sick of this now...
Some other bullshit tax that I probably forgot, or that will be created...			

Table 5: A bit about where the taxes are spent. I use "Bloated Politicians" here to refer to any useless government worker (there are some good ones; not many), as they contribute either directly or indirectly to US politics with their job. See: CBPP

You may not be familiar with terms such as ordinary income or long term capital gains, but that's not the point of this table; what I want you to take away from this table is the atrocious amount of tax you are charged. I have no problem paying money into a system that can benefit my place of residence with great schools, roads and parks, help those in need of financial assistance, and fund protection from actual threats, but this is absolute thievery! You can't even consider taking the stated budget seriously because so much money is wasted in EVERY department; if you have ever dealt with any government agency for permits, construction, military, or literally anything else, you can see the blatant inefficiencies with your own eyes. There are so many bloated, lazy, overpaid, useless people working for the government that sop up this money, both directly and indirectly, who should be fired immediately; many can even be replaced with a computer program. The US Government as a business would fail if it weren't for all of the uneducated, blind lemmings that just accept their current situation in life as immutable and go on overpaying and therefore supporting such an inefficient machine. I absolutely hate having money stolen from me - especially when I sacrifice time with my family to obtain it - and can bitch and moan for 100 pages about how this aspect of the US Government sucks, but I would rather focus my attention on how to pay less tax.

Learning all areas and keeping up with the changing tax rules is a time-consuming task which many don't have the time to do. This is where a great tax professional (CPA) can be very beneficial, even if you use software. Personally, I add CPA expenses like this into my recurring fixed expense budget because I feel that my time is more valuable spent elsewhere than on doing my taxes - that is, after I have found a CPA who I judge to be highly competent and well educated in tax reduction strategies which will not land me in jail, or lead to my assets being seized. A note from personal experience: you don't fuck with the IRS or other tax-collecting agencies.

In order to see how we can legally reduce these taxes, we need to know which ones affect us directly. There are really only 3 main categories of tax in terms of where the money goes: Federal, State, and Local, but looking at them under the lens of subcategories as laid out in the table helps me scrutinize them in a bit more detail. The estate tax doesn't seem to be an issue - if you have $11 million to give, why are you reading this book? - but rather the income taxes, state and local taxes, property taxes, and for some of us who are already investing, capital gains tax. Let's check out each of these and see how they are taken from us, and then see what, if anything, we can do to reduce this.

Income Tax Basics - Federal, State, FICA

Federal tax on income is marginal, meaning it increases in intervals. Your money is cut up into brackets and taxed a certain percentage per bracket. This changes based on your filing status (Single, Married, Head of Household). An income of $100,000 under a filing status of Single would be taxed as follows:

Bracket 1: $9,700 - $0 = $9,700 x 10% = $970
Bracket 2: $39,475 - $9,700 = $29,775 x 12% = $3,573
Bracket 3: $84,200 - $39,475 = $44,725 x 22% = $9,839.50
Bracket 4: $100,000 - $84,200 = $15,800 x 24% = $3,792
Total Federal Income Tax Owed: $970 + $3,573 + $9,839.50 + $3,792 =
$18,174.50

Notice that $9,700 + $29,775 + $44,725 + $15,800 = $100,000

State income tax is dependent on which state your work is performed in, or which state you consider your residence (and can prove) if your work is online. If you live and work in Wyoming (or online), congratulations, you pay $0 in state income tax. If, instead, you live somewhere like Illinois, your state income tax on $100,000 is based on a flat tax of 4.95%, so:

$$\$100,000 \times 4.95\% = \$4,950$$

And lastly, payroll tax, or FICA, is a flat tax based on your gross income. You cannot reduce this tax as an employee, and employers are required to withhold half of it from each paycheck, so you pay 7.65% and your employer pays the other 7.65%. The calculation is straightforward: if you made $100,000 as an employee, your portion of payroll tax is simply:

$$\$100,000 \times 7.65\% = \$7,650$$

Using these calculations in a spreadsheet, or with software will let you know how much to put away each month for that greedy bastard Uncle Sam, which should sit in some type of safe interest bearing account like a high-yield savings. You can then reduce your taxable income using deductions and credits. Being eligible for certain deductions and credits is all rule-based, which is why software and a great CPA are so valuable. Unless you want to visit the IRS website each year to see what has changed before you calculate your estimated tax, just stick to using the calculators on a site like SmartAsset which is regularly updated, use software such as Credit Karma Tax, or ask your CPA to help you.

State and Local Tax

These taxes are applied to things you buy where you live, and most online retail marketplaces add them on when you enter your shipping address. Each state has a different amount, as seen in the table. Reducing these taxes seems to be easiest if you just don't buy stuff. But that's not an option for most of us, so just be smart when/where you shop and know that when you buy new instead of at some used marketplace (garage sale, estate sale, second hand store, dumpster diving, etc…) you are always going to pay more, both in taxes and newness glamour (I think I might copyright this phrase; it's fabulous).

Property Tax

Like state and local tax, this is also dependent on where you live. No matter if you are renting, or looking to buy, property tax affects you. Where I live, depending literally on which side of the street you choose, you will pay either substantially more or less property tax for the same type of property. When you go to rent, landlords (most likely) factor the property tax into their investment, and price the rents accordingly. If you can tick off all the amenities you need in a lower property tax area, live there. There are also certain exemptions which can reduce property tax, so talk to a competent real estate professional (real estate tax attorney for example) about each area you are looking to rent or purchase before making the move.

Capital Gains Tax

For those of you who have some money and wish to start investing, this is a tax for you to try and lower. Capital gains tax comes in two flavors: short and long term. You want the long term tax, so holding assets longer than a year usually converts them to this category. If you don't hold onto the asset long enough, the profit from the sale will be taxed under the category of "ordinary income". This is a problem because investments that fall under "ordinary income" such as short term capital gains are taxed based on your highest federal tax bracket, and may even push you up into a higher bracket, whereas income that is considered long term capital gains is taxed at a fixed rate of either 0%, 15%, or 20%; it is still based on your income, but you will pay 0% if your total income, including the capital gain, is less than $40,000 a year, and 15% if your total income is less than $500,000 per year. From this we can see that shifting our source of income from ordinary to capital gains can be advantageous, which is why owning real estate is a great way to make income. You have your tenant pay you rent, which is taxed as ordinary income, but depreciation from the property along with other tax deductions can reduce this by quite a bit, and you sell sometime after 2 years and voila, you make profit that isn't subject to FICA bullshit, and the federal tax rate is probably lower than what you would pay making $100,000 a year at a job. You can even convert the property into your primary residence (live in one of the rooms/units) or defer tax by using a 1031 exchange (see: How to Prevent a Tax Hit When Selling a Rental Property).

Deductions vs Credits

Deductions are things which lower your taxable income amount, while credits lower your tax due amount directly. To illustrate this, let's consider the median US income of $61,937. If we take the Federal standard deduction of $12,200 (2019 rate), our taxable income is reduced to $61,937 - $12,200 = $49,737. Our Federal tax is then based on that amount, which was calculated for Mary in Chapter 2 as $6,801. Now let's assume Mary has 2 children under age 17; she would then qualify for a tax credit of $1,000 per child, so $2,000. Her Federal tax bill would then be lowered by $2,000 to $4,801. Do you see the difference? The standard deduction reduced the income, making the taxable amount less, while the credit directly reduced her Federal tax bill by the amount of the credit. It gets better: there are refundable credits which, if your tax bill is $0, will actually put money in your pocket.

Let's now look at an example of how employees are taxed versus business entities:

The Employee

As an employee you are able to reduce your income tax, both Federal and State, by taking deductions, qualifying for credits, and having a filing status such as head of household. Additionally, if you contribute your investment or retirement portion of your budget each paycheck to something like a 401K retirement plan, you will be able to write off up to $19,500 as of 2020 on your taxes, some employers even match your contribution (free money), and you may be eligible for the Savers Tax credit. You can look at the actual tax forms that you need to file, such as a 1040 to see which deductions and credits may be available to you and then compare your itemized deductions to the standard deduction for the year to see which is greater. You can also visit the deductions and credits page on the IRS website to go through questionnaires to see which ones you qualify for. You cannot reduce the FICA tax of 7.65% on your gross wage amount as an employee, other than making less money, but why would you want to do that?

The Independent Contractor VS Corporation (LLC)

It seems that America was built for informed business owners. I say this because of all the benefits afforded to a business in the form of tax breaks. When you own a business, there are a couple of ways you can structure yourself, in terms of business entities for tax purposes. You can be an independent contractor, such as an UBER driver, or real estate agent, or set yourself up as a company such as an LLC which can elect to be treated as an S Corporation. "Okay, so enough with the fancy mumbo jumbo"...where are the tax breaks you ask? Well, since I like to tell stories, let's consider one involving two characters: The Independent Plumber Ivan and the S Corporation Plumber Sam. These two guys run the exact same type of business in Illinois and both bring in $100,000 a year - so many people breaking their pipes with excessive toilet paper usage I guess - and have the exact same amount of business expenses, namely $10,000, so they both decided to take the standard deduction of $12,200 (2019 rate). When Ivan goes to pay taxes, here is what his look like:

Federal: $100,000 - $12,200 (federal standard deduction) = $87,800 x all tax brackets = **$15,247**
State: $100,000 - $2275 (IL state standard deduction) = $97,725 x 4.95% = **$4,837**
FICA: $100,000 x 15.3% = **$15,300**

Total Income Tax Owed: $15,247 + $4837 + $15,300 **= $35,384**

Because Sam is treated as an S Corporation, he is able to take a "reasonable salary," which is kind of ambiguous, but for plumbers, the median salary in 2018 was $53,910 according to USNEWS, so we will consider that reasonable, and then pay himself the remaining amount as a distribution. What is deemed reasonable is often the median income for the type of work performed, along with a few other factors, and should be verified by a tax professional. Nevertheless, we will go with that number. His income is split up into two portions, Employee and Distribution, and his taxes look like this:

Employee pay: $53,910 + Distribution pay: $46,090 = $100,000

Federal: $100,000 - $12,200 (federal standard deduction) =

$87,800 x all tax brackets = **$15,247**
State: $100,000 - $2275 (IL state standard deduction) =
$51,635 x 4.95% = **$4,837**
FICA (only on Employee pay): $53,910 x 15.3% = **$8,248**

Total Income Tax Owed: $15,247 + $4,837 + $8,248 = **$28,332**

That is a savings of $7,052!

This is one of the main reasons to go into business for yourself; you can save more money on tax than is possible as an employee, and you normally make more than an employee would. For shits and giggles lets see how the S Corporation stacks against a plumber employed by a company who makes the same gross income of $100,000:

Federal: $100,000 - $12,200 (federal standard deduction) =
$87,800 x all tax brackets = **$15,247**
State: $100,000 - $2275 (IL state standard deduction) =
$97,725 x 4.95% = **$4,837**
FICA: $100,000 x 7.65% = **$7,650**

Total Income Tax Owed: $15,247 + $4837 + $7,650 = **$27,734**

It looks like the employee making the same amount with the same generic write offs will bring home a bit more than Sam with his S Corporation setup, BUT, this situation is practically non-existent because out of two companies offering the same service, the company who has an employee perform it will need to pay the employee less to keep the company alive. This is in addition to the fact that what you can write off as a business vs an employee is extremely different. Having a business opens up the possibility to claim things as depreciable assets that you never could dream of doing as an employee, such as a big screen tv, car, badass computer, dope office, and so on as long as you have all the documentation to back it up AND it complies with IRS rules. Now you can see that American prosperity seems to be biased towards business owners. You may even be able to start a side business for your hobby and claim write offs and losses that could offset income taxes you owe from your regular 9-5. Instead of buying your dream home recording studio with your after-tax-raped McDonald's salary dollars, start a recording business and write it off! I won't get into the fees involved with starting and maintaining an entity such as an S Corp, but it's as simple as creating a spreadsheet and running the numbers to see if it's right for you; talk to a cpa to find out what those numbers are for your area.

Chance of IRS Audit

The general population is usually not aware of any of this tax stuff. Go up to a random person and ask them to calculate the taxes they will pay in that year, or what the chance is of being audited and they probably won't know where to begin. Luckily for them, the standard deduction has been increased to such a high number they don't have to worry about itemizing and its increase to audit risk, but for a business it helps to keep track of everything. If you do decide to create a business for your startup YouTube venture, here are a couple tidbits to further encourage you: The chance of being audited as an S Corporation in 2016 was **0.3%**. This number does not reflect the chance of YOUR S CORP being audited because that calculation requires using Bayes' Theorem and relies on how many red flags YOUR S CORP has in its filing, as compared to the ones that were audited. This is also historical data, meaning that the IRS may increase or decrease this amount in coming years. The rate seems to be decreasing though, at least for individuals. I personally don't worry about getting audited. I keep all records of everything, pay all taxes owed, and have a great financial team. Additionally, there isn't enough funding to have a human look over every single taxpayer's file, so what are considered red flags are usually programmable - if you have filed your taxes with something like TurboTax or Credit Karma Tax then you should have seen a notice stating they are reviewing your submission for audit risk (red flags) - meaning you can use the power of software to keep you safe. You should not let the possibility of an audit stop you from creating a business, or sleeping at night, if you play by the rules.

Tax Reduction Strategies

The following is a list of ways to reduce taxes, based on what we have covered above:

1) Claim all available deductions and credits to reduce your income tax - federal, state, local and payroll - including retirement contributions,

the purchase of wealth generating assets such as real estate, your dependents, etc. You can figure this out with FREE software such as [Credit Karma Tax](), or by working with a great CPA.

2) If you can work for yourself, even as a side hustle, look into starting a business entity such as an S Corporation. If you are a sole proprietor, converting to this should be very beneficial in reducing taxes, as shown above with the plumbers.

3) Stay healthy! This will reduce spending on insurance premiums, deductibles, pills, unnecessary treatments, and so forth. This will also reduce your shopping and food bills because you won't have a gigantic, disgusting, earth destroying diet to fund, thereby also reducing sales tax.

4) If you have friends in states with low sales tax, have them shop for you and mail the item to you, buy at garage sales, or look for items that people/businesses throw away in bulk trash. The amount of waste in this country is nauseating, especially when you know that little kids are living on actual trash dumps in parts of the world that collect US waste, so this has an added benefit of helping the world, in addition to saving on tax.

5) If you can, live in an area with lower property and state tax. For example, If you are unfortunate enough to live in Illinois like I currently am, look for areas which are unincorporated since they usually have way cheaper property tax, or move to a state with zero state taxes and low property taxes, such as Wyoming. More and more employees are working remotely these days, so I don't feel overly silly mentioning this.

6) Reduce Capital Gains tax by investing using strategies that also minimize taxes, such as tax-loss harvesting, real estate, and asset location (not the same as allocation). See chapter 5 for more info, as well as this article on [Investopedia]().

7) This only applies to people who have money to give, but don't be a

dumbass when giving someone a lump sum of money. Spread it out using the yearly gift amount. Look into setting up a trust or company entity to keep assets in the family such as an LLC.

8) Work with a supremely knowledgeable financial team of CPAs, lawyers, and advisors because getting fucked by the IRS is extremely painful and can cause you more financial ruin than paying the tax, even though the audit risk may be low. Is the loop-jumping bullshit? Absolutely, but it is a necessary evil until the US reforms its despicable tax amounts.

My intent with this chapter was to get you to realize that you can become wealthier through saving money on taxes by knowing about some of the "loopholes". Many investors chase a consistent net return on investment of 4%-10%, when taxes can easily take over 40% of your income - according to the congressional budget office, revenue from taxes was 3.5 trillion, while total wages earned was 8.7 trillion (source: FRED) - and it's not as variable as investment return! I hope that this chapter spurs an interest in you to seek out all of the tax benefits that you can qualify for. Don't expect to become wealthy just by reducing your tax bill, rather, realize it is a part of the puzzle and helps you keep more of what you earn. You must increase pay AND keep as much as possible to increase the odds of becoming wealthy. I want to pay taxes, but in the amount of 4%-10%, not 40%, and not on starting an unnecessary war with other countries, shitty government employees, or government debt from poor choices... the list goes on and on…

More Money Math

Just know that you can become wealthy without understanding complex math, but it's something you should absolutely know, as many unscrupulous companies and financial advisors can make it seem like your investments with them are safe because they flop out some fancy math terms to you. Being in the dark about math opens up the possibility of being robbed of your hard earned cash by smooth talkers, so let's shed the mindset that math is impossible to learn and put on our thinking caps. We will start off very simply with the topic of simple versus compound interest, then discuss what inflation is and see how it is calculated (and how to compare stated returns of an investment with tax and inflation adjusted returns).We will finish off with a discussion on probability and simulations to see how we can create a diversified investment portfolio, and a brief intro to the subject of risk analysis. If you couldn't guess, this last portion of the chapter is for those among you who already have a math background and want to see applications in finance and programming - actually useful if you are bored and/or don't want to use a robo-advisor. This should not be considered as investing advice, just speculation and a bit of fun. I personally only invest what I can lose financially and mentally. Thinking you will become wealthy overnight from investing in the stock market, or any other investment, is no different than thinking you will become wealthy by gambling at a casino. Once you accept that you can lose it all in any investment, the money allotted to the activity should not exceed what you can and would budget for any other fun, fleeting activity (eating at restaurants, movies, Starbucks). There are multiple long historical periods (we will see) which show to be profitable for those investing in such things as the stock market, which is why I have included investing in my budget, as well as here. If there is a possibility to make money from investing, I think it can be considered an addition to the probability of becoming wealthy, but only when proceeding cautiously and using history as a guide.

Simple VS Compounding Interest

You can earn interest, or you can pay interest. But that's not all - you can even earn or pay interest on interest! I recommend earning interest, but this is

America so we will take a look at paying interest (just pretend the interest is owed to you and not the bank if you want to see how much an investment can bring in). We will look at both formulas to see how much money can be made or lost to interest, which should help you when making financial decisions such as which type of loan to get, the length of time to keep money in the stock market, and so on.

Simple interest is just the amount of money that accrues on the original amount of money, or principal, as it's referred to by people in suits. This is the formula for simple interest:

Simple Interest = Principal x Interest Rate x Length of Time

Oftentimes you will see letters in place of each thing (called a variable in math), but it is all the same. Let's check out an example:

You have taken out a $1,000 loan at a 10% interest rate with a 5 year length of time. To see how much you will owe in simple interest, we simply fill out the formula:

Principal = $1,000 | Interest Rate = 10%, or 0.10 | Length of Time = 5 years

Simple Interest = 1000 x 0.10 x 5 = $500

Therefore, you will pay $1,500 for something you wanted for $1,000. Stupid, right? But it gets even more stupid with compound interest. Here is the formula:

Compound interest = $P[(1+i/n)^{nt} - 1]$

where:
P = Principal
i = interest rate in percentage terms
n = number of compounding periods per year
t = total number of years for the investment or loan

If we fill these variables in with the same values used in the simple interest calculation we get:

$P = \$1{,}000 \mid i = 10\%, \text{ or } 0.10 \mid n = 1 \mid t = 5$

Compound interest $= 1000 \times [(1+0.10/1)^{5*1} - 1] = 1000 \times 0.61051 = \$610.51$

Now the item you want to purchase for $1,000 will cost you $1,610.51! This is how you lose money fast.

If you are thinking, "wow, this is super stupid!" here is another rediculously stupid fact about compounding interest (when you are paying it): The number of compounding periods per year has a strong effect on the amount of money you will have in interest. Why? Well, that variable is in the exponent spot, meaning it has a large influence on the formula. Above, we used a compounding period of 1, but a more realistic compounding rate can be found in the fine print of credit card agreements. The good folks over at Experian have gone through an example which I will similarly lay out here:

Suppose you want to buy that same stupid item from the above two examples for $1,000, but you were turned down for a loan at the bank. You Google "Apply for Credit Cards" and apply for the first one you see (very bad idea), and without reading the interest rate terms, you go buy your $1,000 item on the first day of January because, hey, it's a new year and you want to look fab. The problem starts that day. The credit card you used charges interest DAILY on your average daily balance. The credit card company charges 25% per year, so to figure out how much interest daily we divide 25% by the amount of days in a year: 0.25/365 = 0.0006849315. This means that on January 1st your balance is $1,000, then on January 2nd your balance is $1,000 + $1,000 x 0.0006849315 = $1000.6849315, and on January 3rd the balance is now $1000.6849315 + $1000.6849315 x 0.0006849315 = $1001.37033213 … and to figure out your balance on January 31st, we use the compounding interest formula with some minor tweaks:

$P = \$1{,}000 \mid i = 0.25 \mid n = 365 \mid t = 31/365$ (convert years to days)

Balance on Jan 31st $= 1000 \times [(1+0.0006849315)^{31}] = 1000 \times 1.02145247379 = \$1021.45$

And if you don't pay it off, but instead pay the $10 minimum payment, here is what it looks like at the end of the year:

Balance Starting February = January's balance - minimum payment = $1011.45

Balance on Feb 30th = $1011.45 \times [(1+0.0006849315)^{30}]$ = 1011.45 x 1.02075332768 = $1032.44
Mar = $1044.37 | Apr = $1055.84 | May = $1,068.28
Jun = $1,080.24 | July = $1,093.20 | Aug = $1,106.44
Sept = $1,119.19 | Oct = $1,132.98 | Nov = $1,146.29
Dec = $1,160.67

Continuing this way we have a balance at the end of the year (with rounding) of $1,160.67, and don't forget the $120 in minimum monthly payments you spent, bringing the total to $1,280.67 for a $1,000 item. Comparing this to simple interest, we would have $1000 + $1000 x 0.25 = $1,250. This example used a credit card interest rate, but even using the same interest rate as the first two examples of 10%, a term length of 5 years, and assuming $0 in monthly payments, we would have:

P = $1,000 | i = 0.10 | n = 365 | t = 5
Daily Compounded Interest = $1000 \times [(1+0.0002739726)^{1825} - 1]$ = 1000 x 0.64860836083 = $648.61

Simple Interest = $500   Yearly Compounded Interest = $610.51   Daily Compounded Interest = $648.61

This is a difference of **$148.61 for a $1,000 purchase** between daily compounded interest and simple interest, at the same interest rate! I hope this shows you that it is very important to your wallet which type of interest you will be paying or earning. If you want to read more about these topics, check out this article at Investopedia or head over to Money Chimp to read about how interest formulas are used in investments such as bonds. This is semi-complicated math, and requires some knowledge about theorems and proofs to really grasp what is going on (instead of simply memorizing formulas, which any chimp can do). Building wealth doesn't need to be that complicated, so here is a heuristic, or rule of thumb: Don't borrow money... but if you *have* to otherwise you would die, make sure you understand how they charge interest and know how much money you will be losing. I think that just this information alone would stop many people from using credit cards, but many don't take the time to see how the math of their spending works out in favor of the debt holder, not them.

Inflation

When you hear the term inflation, do you think of something growing in size? If you said yes, then that is just the right image to have in your head for the meaning of inflation in finance. The cost of goods and services changes price for some reason, **[insert your favorite economic theory here]** and we keep track of the amount with a measuring device called the Consumer Price Index, or CPI, because acronyms are all the rage. The CPI tracks things like haircuts, clothing, housing prices and groceries using a survey method, according to the second FAQ: *How is the CPI market basket determined?* on bls.gov. Additionally, the CPI is a number that is relative to inflation back in 1984, at which point the CPI was set to 100, so if CPI is currently 110 that means average prices on goods and services have gone up 10% relative to prices in 1984. I have a couple comments before we continue. First, surveys are absolute shit when it comes to data collection - is your memory of what you spent on gas last week reliable? Mine's not - and Second, this is an averaged number that may or may not be close to the actual prices in your town. Is the CPI even useful then? Well, it's a place to start, and prices do increase over the years so it is a good calculation to know when you are planning on calculating retirement spending. This is a very simple calculation:

Inflation = [(index now - index in the past)/ index in the past] x 100
Example: (110-108)/108 x 100 = 1.85%

Here is one more example - factoring inflation into your investment return:

Inflation Adjusted Return = [(1 + investment return) / (1 + inflation rate)] - 1

This formula accounts for the compounding that takes place in investing and inflation. So, if you had a 10% investment return and the inflation was 1.85%, and both compounded annually, your inflation adjusted return would be:

Inflation Adjusted Return = [(1 + 0.10) / (1 + 0.0185)] - 1 = 8%

This number means that life, on average, is more expensive now than in the past. This is also why letting your cash sit in a savings account that earns practically 0% return may not be the best thing to do. Inflation is used in all sorts of calculations and decisions by economists and the government, but for someone trying to build wealth I think it is just important to be aware of the rising cost of goods and services. Simply spending less on bullshit and more on lowish-risk wealth generating assets may help limit the damage inflation can cause on your money. Obviously if you buy a financial asset and its price drops, it may reduce your purchasing power even more than inflation, so a high yield savings or CD when the rates go back up, might be a good place for money to sit if you don't want to risk losing it.

Probability

Life is all a big guess to us because we are not [Laplace's Demon](); we don't know the future of practically anything. I like to guess using the math of probability, and even though it's based on past events, it's the best we have, or at least I think so. Here I will define the probability of an event simply as: Total # of ways an event can occur / Total events possible. I'm defining probability in this way to try and sidestep the correctness debate between Frequentist and Bayesian statisticians, and I don't know much about infinity; if you don't know what I'm talking about, check out [THIS]() MIT document. I will be cliche here and choose a die as an example. There are six sides to a die numbered 1,2,3,4,5 and 6 respectively. If I ask you what the probability of rolling one die and obtaining a 6 is, all you need to do is recognize there is only 1 side that will give you a 6 out of the six sides. So the probability of the event: rolling a 6 = 1/6. Side Note: This is as good as it gets for humans, because the outcome doesn't just depend on the number of sides, but the velocity at which you toss the die, the air density, the side that was up initially, and an almost infinite amount of other factors. What if we add another die and are now playing dice? I ask the question again, but this time you have two dice working for you. Now we would like to ask ourselves how many different ways there are for the two dice to equal 7 out of all of the totals they could equal. We need a table:

	Die 2 Could Be					
Die 1 Could Be	1	2	3	4	5	6
1	2	3	4	5	6	7
2	3	4	5	6	7	8
3	4	5	6	7	8	9
4	5	6	7	8	9	10
5	6	7	8	9	10	11
6	7	8	9	10	11	12

Table 6: The tan column on the left represents the possible states of die 1, and the green row above the top represents the possible states of die 2. The light blue area in the center is every sum of the dice possible. Gold was used to highlight a sum of 7.

What we are looking at is all possible combinations of the two dice. As highlighted in gold (because a 7 will win you some gold at the casino) we see that there are six different events that add up to a 7: 1+6, 2+5, 3+4, 4+3, 5+2, 6+1. Since die 1 and die 2 can be either a 1 or a 6, they give us more possible events than rolling one die. Looking at the blue section, including the gold 7's, we see that there are a total of 36 different events. Our probability of rolling a 7 is 6/36, or ⅙, just like rolling a 6 with one die. This is actually the most generous probability in the table, so thanks casinos, you may have a heart after all.

To see how this applies to making money, we think of events in life that generate wealth: getting an education, networking, saving, investing, buying second hand, starting a business and so on. There could be many ways to reach each event, but we can think of each of them as having a 1/2 probability of creating wealth; they either do or don't. Thus, the total probability of creating wealth is the sum of all events we can think of which create wealth, or 1/2 + 1/2 + 1/2 +1/2 + 1/2 +1/2 = 3, divided by the total # of events in the universe. Just kidding… The way I actually think about probability when total events are incalculable is through developed intuition, not necessarily a math formula, but if it were a math formula it would look like Bayes' Theorem because I'm just picking probabilities to go along with my personal experiences. I know through experience that spending money loses money and saving keeps it, so saving would be a wealth generating event. Investing is a bit more tricky because I don't know if it will generate wealth or if I will lose everything, which is why a guess must be made, call it educated if you will, but a guess nonetheless. My previous career was writing children's books about cats in hats and foxes wearing sox… I'm so funny… Back to probability. As I said, we don't know the future so all we can do is try and make a guess about what generates wealth based on observations and data and do as many of those things as possible. I used the number 7 above because that was the "break even" number for two dice, meaning rolling a 7 with two dice is the same probability as rolling a 1-6 on one die. Once you add a third die, the probability of rolling a 7 is reduced to 15/216 or 7%, just like losing in the next investment made. This all seems too abstract so I'm going back to basics: If we think there are 1000 things we can do that are related to money, both losing and earning, doing as many of the money earning things out of the 1000 things we could do gives us a higher probability of becoming wealthy (this is of course subjective, but if you have a better idea please get ahold of me). And so, landing a great career, having a high level of education, saving money, and investing should boost the probability of obtaining wealth. I feel like I have made my point and am now grinding my pencil into a stubby, useless chunk of yellow-coated wood (even though I typed this).

Investing - Adjusted Returns

Disclaimer: Investing in ANYTHING, even the "low-risk" stuff can be more risky than a calculation says. WHY? Because the calculation is based on historical data of human behaviour and other economic factors which can be wildly unpredictable. Check out my video: [How Investing Can Kill You](#)

When investing, make sure you are comparing apples to apples and not to watermelons. You need to know what the real historical numbers are for each investment you choose, including fees, taxes, and if the numbers shown on the investment advertisement adjust for inflation or not, as well as the calculated risk (but it's not a guarantee of future risk). To illustrate this we are going to compare stock market items: Wealthfront and Vanguard stated performances on particular assets held. I would love to include real estate landlording and flipping in this comparison, but readily available historical performance mainly captures home value and rent fluctuation and leaves out much needed details that eat your potential profit: property management fees, HOA, property tax, tenant destruction by meth lab, tenant not paying and so forth. Some of these variables can be looked up for a particular area you are interested in, while others, such as probability of non-payment, or tenant destruction by meth lab cannot easily be found. If I discussed the real estate investments I've made, that would only serve as a personal anecdote which is regarded as very weak evidence, so I'll skip that, but feel free to watch these two videos about real estate investing: [Real Estate Investing - Leveraging Money](#) and (my preferred way) [Finding Residential Rentals](#). Additionally, conventional real estate investing has a super high price to entry, making it an almost impossible investment for most starting their wealth building journey. And so, we will stick to stock market gambling (the stock market does have REITs though, if you *must* have a piece of real estate action). On Vanguard's site you can find their Total Stock Market Index Fund ([VTSAX](#)) which gives you exposure to all stocks in the stock market. You simply buy a share of VTSAX and then you reap the profits and losses from every stock available in the market. Wealthfront on the other hand is a fancy shmancy automated portfolio creator which just asks you how risk seeking or averse you are, then creates a mix of assets accordingly using things like Government Bonds which are considered low risk, stocks which are considered high risk, real estate and natural resources, and tries to optimize your portfolio through various tax reduction strategies. VTSAX has a risk potential of 4, and I couldn't find how Vanguard or Wealthfront calculate their risk numbers exactly, so to try and find a similarly risky investment on Wealthfront, I will convert Wealthfront's risk scores by dividing them by 2 since they go from 0.5 to 10.0. And so, to get a similar risk potential as VTSAX we will choose a Wealthfront portfolio with a risk score of 8. Yes, VTSAX is all stocks, while a Wealthfront portfolio is a mix of mainly stocks and bonds, but a similar risk score should put them on similar grounds I would think. Risk is a calculation based on historical data and involves the probability of losing money, but we will talk about it later. For now, just think the higher the risk number, the higher the chance of losing money. Ok, enough words, let's check out some pictures:

No Money, No Stuff

ASSET CLASS	Taxable account		Retirement account	
	TAX DRAG	NET-OF-FEE, AFTER-TAX RETURN	TAX DRAG	NET-OF-FEE, AFTER-TAX RETURN
US Stocks	1.0%	4.7%	0.8%	4.9%
Foreign Developed Stocks	1.1%	5.0%	0.8%	5.3%
Emerging Market Stocks	1.2%	6.1%	0.7%	6.5%
Dividend Stocks	0.9%	4.0%	0.7%	4.1%
Natural Resources	1.0%	4.8%	0.6%	5.2%
Real Estate	1.7%	5.4%	0.8%	6.2%
US Government Bonds	0.9%	2.0%	0.6%	2.2%
TIPS	1.1%	2.2%	0.7%	2.6%
Municipal Bonds	0.3%	2.4%	0.6%	2.1%
US Corporate Bonds	1.2%	2.4%	0.7%	2.9%
Emerging Market Bonds	1.6%	3.6%	0.7%	4.5%
Risk Parity	1.5%	4.5%	0.9%	5.1%

Table 4: Snapshot taken from Wealthfront's White Paper

Wealthfront's average annual net-of-fees, pre-tax returns
Last updated on 07/31/2020

Risk Score 8.0	1 YEAR RETURN	3 YEAR RETURN	5 YEAR RETURN	SINCE INCEPTION
Taxable portfolios Personal, Joint, and Trust accounts	4.16%	5.58%	6.43%	7.41% Since 10/14/2011
Tax-advantaged portfolios Roth, Traditional, and SEP IRAs	5.07%	6.14%	6.97%	8.36% Since 10/14/2011

Read historical performance disclosure

Table 5: Snapshot taken from: https://www.wealthfront.com/historical-performance

43

After-tax returns—updated quarterly
as of 06/30/2020

	1-yr	3-yr	5-yr	10-yr	Since inception 11/13/2000
Total Stock Mkt Idx Adm					
Returns before taxes	6.45%	10.03%	10.02%	13.73%	6.80%
Returns after taxes on distributions	5.95%	9.52%	9.50%	13.24%	6.38%
Returns after taxes on distributions and sales of fund shares	4.12%	7.74%	7.84%	11.46%	5.60%

Table 6: Snapshot taken from:
https://investor.vanguard.com/mutual-funds/profile/performance/vtsax

In Chapter 2 I said a 10% return compounded annually year over year is difficult to obtain, and here you can see why. The 5 year **net of fee, after-tax** return on VTSAX blows Weathfront's **net of fee, pre-tax** return out of the water, but that is just a snapshot of 5 specific years ending on 6/30/2020, and it is not as diversified - in terms of asset classes - as Wealthfront's portfolio. Generally, the longer the time in an investment (known as time horizon), along with diversification, the less you are affected by extreme ups and downs. We can see that since inception, VTSAX **net of fee, after-tax** return is 5.60%, while the **net of fee, after-tax** return for Wealthfront's portfolio with a risk score of 8 is not prominently displayed (most likely due to differing tax situations and tax-loss harvesting). The only thing I could find was their hypothesized **net of fee, after-tax** return on each asset class, and it looks like 6.1% on Emerging Market Stocks was highest. Holding Emerging Market Stocks alone would correspond to a risk score of around 10, meaning any mix of asset classes should have a **net of fee, after-tax** return less than or equal to 6.1% at Wealthfront. Let's not stop here though. Looking at the data for 20 year returns on stocks, we can also see that gaining a 10% return compounded year over year in the stock market (well, the S&P 500) is a pipe dream, especially after adjusting for fees, taxes and inflation. The way we do this is to look at each 20 year period possible starting from a particular month and year in which the data was available - this is known as calculating a rolling return - then calculate a probability of having a 10% or higher return out of all of the returns calculated. As a math formula it looks like this:

$$P(20RR >= 10\%) = \frac{\text{\# of x year periods with 10\% return or higher}}{\text{Total \# of x year returns}}$$

Where: $P(20RR >= 10\%)$: probability of any 20 year S&P 500 return being equal or greater than 10%

In order to try and account for times of disaster, we would like to have the rolling returns include those data points which reflect such times (Panics, Depressions, Recessions, Black Monday's, Covid Crisis, etc...). We can use monthly return data from the S&P 500 stock index which covers January of 1871 to August 2020, and includes dividends and inflation (source: Shiller Data). I first calculated the number of shares one would have after 20 years of monthly dividend reinvestment, then multiplied that by the selling price at the 20 year mark, subtracted the purchase price, and finally, divided the entire thing by the purchase price. It looks like this:

$$20\ Year\ Total\ Return\ =\ \frac{(\#\ of\ shares\ after\ 20\ years\ x\ Sell\ Price) - Purchase\ Price}{Purchase\ price}$$

See my Google Sheet Here: My Google Sheet Calculations

After finding the 20 year total return, I used the compound formula from above to solve for an average annual return. This number is a geometric mean equal to what you would earn each year as a compounded return rate. I found that out of the 1557 months in the dataset, if you were to hold the S&P 500 and reinvest your dividends each month, the probability of obtaining an inflation-adjusted yearly compounding return of 10% or higher was 12.20%. This is before taxes and fees - hence my skepticism of this level of return. A more reasonable return from the S&P 500 with dividends reinvested, based on this data, would be 4-5% compounded annually, as there were over 77% of the 20 year returns which achieved 4% or above. Note that this is for a passive investment where the money does the hard work. You can generate insane returns in business, but that requires your time, tons of skill, and a bunch of luck. The entire point of investing in passive assets is to create other streams of income down the road without sucking your time on a consistent basis. Yes, reading a book or listening to a lecture here and there takes time, but eventually you reach a point where you develop a strategy to set and forget your money and it will hopefully grow without a consistent time investment. Research shows that investors who try and time the market, stock pick, and practice buying and selling based on flag patterns, head and shoulders, inverted dildos and other such voodoo are wasting their time and money. The historical data says that you need to invest in the stock market for the long haul, or you risk losing your money. Of course if this data I used is shit, the conclusions will be as well, so hopefully Mr. Shiller was thorough. Another of course is that this is historical data, and it may not represent the future at all. This is gambling, no question about it.

Portfolio Optimization

There have been tomes of information written on creating the perfect portfolio, and many classes taught on the subject. Here I am going to remain true to my style and KIASAP, or keep it as simple as possible. I have a goal with my money, that is, I want to make it multiply in the quickest time possible. This means I need great return rates, low risk rates, and some luck to avoid money-stealing uncertainty that lurks around every corner (this last bit is probably too much to ask for). How should I approach this problem? With a model created by simulation. This is waaaay more complex than the previous math formulas, and I will not be going into detail here - that level of detail can be found in [Wealthfront's White Paper](). Instead, I want to discuss a high level overview of the process of simulation. If you do want to see how I attempt to code this up, you'll need to subscribe to my YouTube channel [World's Best Guys]() for updates; hey, give me a break, I'm a dad, run multiple businesses, and incessantly exercise, I'll (most likely) be uploading the video someday. If you have zero desire to learn this, just go to a robo advisor such as [Wealthfront](), [SoFi](), [Betterment](), or directly to the source of some high quality ETFs and portfolios at [Vanguard](). Just be aware that any robo advisor will tack on a fee above any costs associated with the asset they purchase for your portfolio - such as ETFs, Bonds, Stocks, etc - so make sure to read the fine print and compare costs and returns as shown in the Investing section of this chapter.

I'm nowhere near the level of floppy math coder that Wealthfront developers claim to be, which is why I just do it for fun. If you think I'm nuts because I consider this fun, you are correct, I'm nuts. Ok, so the first thing a simulation-creating financial planner needs, besides stimulants, is time series data. This is just some values at given points in time (usually 2 columns in a spreadsheet) and can be obtained from places such as yahoo finance, if it's stock data that is needed, or [FDIC]() for CD historical rate of returns, or some other outlet which collects historical data such as [CRSP](). The data is then used to create a probability of some event, say obtaining 10% in the stock market, given all events, or data points available. The amounts of data are usually extremely gigantic, and you saw that with just two dice the table of probability was pretty large, so imagine the insane event probability table needed to illustrate all of this historical data! Hell no, sir. This is where simulations come into play; I ♥ computers! On a very high level, all of the data is analyzed and each outcome is calculated, so if we have 3,700 stocks to pick from, precious metals, or REITs and want to know what percent of our investment to put into each to obtain the most money, we have the computer run all possible combinations of each investment and come up with a portfolio that has the greatest return.

Risk, Uncertainty, and Model Accuracy

The simulation wouldn't be complete just looking for the highest return portfolio though. This is because everything can change depending on which time periods were included in the simulation. We want to try and gather characteristics about each stock, bond, metal or financial asset that we want to include such as variability in price, reaction to economic downturns, and relationship to each other, or correlation. For example, if a Tesla stock sinks and a McDonald's stock rises (negative correlation to each other) when the economy is in the shitter, and we have historical data to (probably shittily) predict when the economy may be in such a place using recession data for example, we would want to use that information in our simulation. Since we don't know what the future holds, we are relying on patterns of behavior. A way to try and combat this is through holding many different assets that seem to be either weakly or completely unrelated in terms of how their price reacts to economic situations. An example of this is an index fund such as Vanguard's Diversified Equity Fund (VDEQX), or VTSAX which we discussed above. This could all be wrong and what we thought were patterns can lead us astray, meaning that McDonald's might go bankrupt, or people will get sick of their fake, nasty "food," driving the price of their stock to zero while, simultaneously, Tesla's overpriced stock goes to zero because no one likes their shitty, weird looking things they call vehicles.

Many of the theories behind portfolio creation and investing involve assumptions about risk and uncertainty. I want to clarify here that when I talk about risk, I am referring to something calculated based on past data, while uncertainty is something that cannot be calculated. Some refer to uncertainty as systematic risk, but I think that just muddies up the distinction. Risk for me is just the probability of losing money, and like any probability, is calculated historically by looking at how the price or return of an asset is distributed (how it fluctuated) over a given period of time; one common assumption is that this distribution is normal which may not be the case, such as the returns of the [S&P 500 since 1950](). The reason for the name "normal distribution" is not exactly known, some think it has to do with it being common in nature (such as the average height of a person or shrub), but all I know is it's a bell-shaped curve, meaning that most of the events inside surround the mean value. This assumption of a normal price distribution makes it mathematically easy to calculate stuff like a standard deviation, which is then used as a component in the assessment of portfolio risk. Considering what the US economy has witnessed in the past 100 years, this normal distribution assumption is being heavily questioned; the loss caused by the great recession, the 2020 Covid chaos, and so forth has basically a zero probability of occurring under this normal distribution, but yet here we are. I would consider the normal distribution of asset risk a heated topic in investing, and will not go much further on the subject here, but it appears that using a variant called a fat-tailed model to base portfolio risk on may be a better idea. If you are mathematically inclined and need more, please see [this journal article]() about fat-tailed distributions in risk models.

Since I have been ending each subsection in this chapter with a heuristic, here is another: Don't invest money you are not willing to lose, financially and emotionally. I think about it this way, if I spend my money on anything that is not a wealth generating asset, I lose it - vacations, cars, food - but with investments that I have tried to make my best guess on, I at least have a chance of making money. If I lose it, I lose it, oh well. As long as the money comes from my budget and I did not borrow money to make the investment, I can only lose the amount I put in. The model generated, or simulated, is only as accurate as its inputs, and we are trying to use the past to predict the future of some behaviour that may or may not repeat. Thus, the model accuracy will fluctuate as time goes on and the future writes itself. This is why my budget uses only a total of 20% of my income on all investments, retirement included. If you don't like to gamble, then you can reduce that to 10% by putting all of your retirement money into a high yield savings account, or something similar. Most people spend over 75% of their income EASILY on stupid shit like too big of a house, financing a car, fancy shoes, clothes, restaurants and so on, so a reduction in spending alone would help them tremendously. When you have 20% recurring debt relative to your income, 20% put aside for investing is pennies; do you cry when you lose pennies? If so, stop paying for so many non-wealth generating assets!

Questions to provoke thought:

1. If interest rates go up, what type of correlation, if any, do they have to inflation? Create a chart comparing them.

2. If interest rates go up, what type of correlation to investments such as CDs, Money Market Accounts, Stocks, etc do they have? Create a chart comparing them.

3. What does an index such as the Case-Shiller National Home Price Index actually tell us about homes? See it here: [Home Price Index](). Do they have any predictive power? If so, what can they predict?

4. Does the housing market have a correlation with the stock market? Can you find correlations between the housing market and another financial asset? Create a chart comparing them.

5. Should you adjust for inflation when your money sits there? I'll give you the answer: Yes, the actual value of the dollar is what matters. Dollars are just green paper symbols with dead people on them. Intrinsically worthless.

6. Economic indicators are often gawked at by both degree-holding economists and armchair economists. Calculate the historic strength of leading and lagging economic indicators in terms of probability of something negative happening in the economy. You can get started with these 10 on [Investopedia]().

7. Which do you trust more with your money and why: human advisor, robo advisor?

8. Model a future inflation amount by finding a best fit line to historic inflation, or incorporating other outside factors in the model. What does your model predict for 5,10,15 years from now? Post that shit on Facebook to show off your awesome math skillz. No one will care, but do it anyways. Add #nomoneynostuff to the post.

9. As mentioned above, I used historic data provided by Robert Shiller to calculate the probability of obtaining a certain return in the S&P 500 stock index. Calculate probabilities for other indices such as Dow Jones, NASDAQ, and other Global market indices.

10. Model the fluctuation of the Federal funds rate - including any other voodoo-licious goodies/variables - to try and predict when CDs, high yield savings, and other "low risk" assets will reach respectable levels again.

11. Which math model(s) do you like to rely on for uncertainty simulations and why? And further, should you use pseudo-random numbers as generated by deterministic algorithms, true random numbers generated by outside events, such as radioactive decay or atmospheric noise, or both in your models?

Minimalism

Minimalism is a buzz word usually ascribed to a trendy, neo-hippie movement of ~~homeless~~ "houseless" people who either live in 80 square foot structures built atop trailers, or considerably more cramped spaces such as vans, and Vlog on YouTube about how sexy and luxurious their lives are. I can't imagine that being the case; body odor or a fart alone will stink your place up for days. I think the reality of living in a tiny home looks more like the life of Ted Kaczynski: no friends, no things, and a manifesto in the works. What I preach about in this book is living a lifestyle that is minimalist compared to one's budget. In other words, living within or below their means. I have nothing against people buying a mansion and Bugatti if it's living in their means, but having the option to live this way doesn't apply to most. What's more, living as a minimalist doesn't create much debt, if any, and it reduces waste because new gadgets, clothes, and other things aren't bought as frequently. Although the tiny house movement is on the extreme end of minimalism, I do think the world as a whole would be a cleaner, healthier place without this greed for more all the time, but that is a personal choice one can exercise when they have the cash to do so. Unfortunately, since humans have pleasure pathways in their brains which are as sensitive to buying shiny new toys as they are to getting high on heroin, I don't see greed going away anytime soon. Oh, and don't fall for how radical minimalism on Social Media currently is - most of those people probably hate their lies... I mean lives. If you want to be an extreme minimalist, try it out, and if it sucks give it up. I'm not here to say that minimalism is the only way to live, but rather that it can be a method of accumulating money.

The idea of living a minimalist life brings up a natural question: what would the economy look like if everyone were to adopt it? Before we tackle that, let me first state my distinction between an economy and economic system. An economic system such as Capitalism, Socialism, Communism, or any other 'ism, is basically a philosophy of resource allocation based on human entitlement, while an economy is the real life process of resource allocation in action. I think we should try out a thought experiment using a simplified foundation and build up to the present so that we don't get caught up in the nuances of economic systems; we will only be concerned with what the economy could look like if everyone were minimalists now. In the beginning, there were people on the earth, well actually there were just the laws of physics in the beginning (or so they say), but we will fast forward a few billion years. Ok, so these primitive people had needs which can be defined as things required to keep people alive: food, water, and shelter. You could also make the case for relationships, but I won't. Everything else, it seems to me, is a want. Now, when the population density of an area is low everyone who is physically capable should be autonomous, meaning they should be able to take care of their own needs, especially under the guidance of the elderly - which is why you always go mushroom picking with an old person, but that is a story for another book - and therefore a formal economic system is pretty much unnecessary. Each person governs themselves, and if they don't, they die. Simple. As time goes on these people copulate - or "bang" for the less biologically savvy - the male and female banging leads to little people and, before you know it, there are people everywhere. This primitive population then begins to understand more about the world because their brains have evolved to be badass puzzle solvers and we get tools, agriculture, and better housing which we'll collectively refer to as STUFF. Prior to this there were just autonomous people chillin 'and living within their means; because means were just based on what you could make for yourself, it's kind of hard to live outside of them. Now, due to the density and creation of STUFF, there are serious comparisons being made. A villager named Joe sees another villager named Jon build a super nice house out of mud which is way better than Joe's hole, and it has a roof, so Joe becomes green with envy. Since evolution is driven by natural selection, and we live in a cold cold world, Joe has a brain that wishes to kill, enslave, exploit and consume beyond what he needs to survive. So Joe kills Jon and takes his house and female. Joe sees other local people with STUFF he doesn't have, but there are many of them, so Joe gets together a couple other envious guys to form a plan. The plan is to make the people's lives depend on Joe and his gang, so Joe is now in a position to take STUFF and dictate with force what types of activities can go on, as well as who gets what. It is during this time that the birth of a formal economic system occurs. There is now a social divide between people: slaves to Joe's rule and the people in Joe's Government, a.k.a. politicians. Because minimalism is based on means in this book, minimalism has a different look depending on who is being scrutinized. Slave means are not much, and minimalism for them is basically all they have. If they tried to overstep their situation they would be killed, so that isn't too popular an option. Joe and his politicians on the other hand don't really have means because they are the rulers. To reduce the abstraction and bring us closer to my idea of minimalism, we need a money system, so poof, a money system is formed. The politicians are the ones using money so they can start assigning relative value to their various roles. Slaves are still slaves, and their lives suck, but now means, and therefore minimalism, becomes more of an applicable concept due to a wage.

The density of the population and invention of STUFF continues. Traditions give rise to wants that are increasingly thought of as needs, which in turn is passed down through the generations of politicians; slaves are just trying to stay alive at this point. Note that neither needs nor resources have changed from the primitive beginning of the story. The powerful humans have just created a formal way to make others act to satisfy their wants, and since brains get addicted to power and STUFF, the social gap continues to widen. Eventually Joe dies and the new, hip ruler gets rid of slavery and instead decides to pay the former slaves for their production work, but it's a tiny amount which he decides to call minimum wage. Now everyone has purchasing power, but we are still missing one thing to bring us into our current American economy. Credit. No one knows what the fuck it means or where it came from, but the I OWE YOU has just been formed. With the invention of credit both the rich and the poor now have the ability to live beyond their means. Some of the poor people head to a car dealership where they hear that they can trade in their horse for a machine that puts out the power of 15 horses, all for an "affordable" monthly payment. Word reaches the masses and before you know it everyone is working 24/7 to pay all these bills for STUFF. Of course the rich own the dealership so they just keep getting richer, and the poor get more poor with their terrible spending habits. With this foundation laid we can revisit the original question, namely, what the economy would look like if everyone were a minimalist. Well, it would look just fine. People would survive just like they did in the past, and there would be a much lower wage gap. Why? Because the purchase of STUFF on credit would stop, reducing profits of giant companies, and outsourcing of services would be unnecessary because producers and consumers in the local economy would be more inclined to strike up an agreeable deal. The problems in an economy seem to arise when people become greedy and want more STUFF, leaving the minimalist way of life. This eventually seems to culminate in debt and war.

I think one of America's biggest economic flaws is allowing an unsustainable debt economy. I think this for the simple reason that those who tend to get themselves in debt don't suddenly experience a change in character. There is a robbery of Peter to pay Paul, and Peter just bought a shotgun so we know shit is about to go down. Currently in 2020, many Americans have so many wants that they get themselves, and everyone else, into extreme debt chasing after them. I included everyone else because consumption drives the price of goods and services up for all consumers. This is a vicious cycle that widens the socioeconomic gap to the point of riots, class wars, and destructive demonstrations, and has fueled the idea that a Capitalist economic system is inherently evil and should be immediately shunted in favor of something like Socialism. Many millennials are growing up with this notion that America = Capitalism = Satan, but as we saw in Chapter 4, we give back A TON of money to Uncle Sam which is distributed in a Socialistic way, so I'd say it's time to update that belief. If you hate Capitalism, don't buy a bunch of shit; live as an extreme minimalist in a cardboard box. Capitalism's success is the result of consumerism. I personally love the idea of Capitalism because it allows one to change their status, even if they weren't born into the oligarchy. There is currently so much opportunity in America to change your socioeconomic class regardless of race, religion, or sexual identification. If you don't believe this, consider the fact that transgender bathrooms were created. This is NO DOUBT due to a privately owned business not wanting to lose profit, a.k.a. Capitalism. Having the opportunity to choose how you live is awesome, and you basically get that in America.

In the end, the best economic system is the one that... well... there is no best economic system, especially for a nihilistic-leaning individual like me. There is only my opinion vs your opinion, and the "correct" system is one which survives. There are aspects of conventional economic systems I like, and ones I don't. I wish the American Government didn't interfere so much with business, and charged way less tax, but overall I am happy to have so many opportunities available, and so many loopholes to use. My desire to live a minimalist life reduces my need to make more money than I already do because I could care less about accumulating shit, which ironically makes me wealthier. Not buying stuff allows my money to pile up in savings and investments, and so, minimalism for me is a wealth generating event and should be strongly considered as a factor in the probability of increasing one's wealth.

A Wealth of Mindsets

Nature favors the clever and brave, as bravery alone didn't always stop tigers and other man-eating beasts from killing people.

Do nothing less than what it takes to bring in money. Right and wrong are relative to your position on the social ladder.

Look for opportunities to make more money where you currently are. Look elsewhere as well.

America was founded by murdering thieves who then set up a government that benefited their families. The term "by the people, for the people" probably doesn't include you or your family.

People who tell you to play by the rules are either weak or too powerful and want to remain that way.

Don't chase get rich quick schemes. They are making the guy at the top of the pyramid rich, not you.

If it seems too good to be true, walk away. This includes spending money on seminars and guru webinars, as well as anything that includes the phrase "my system".

Buy stuff according to your budget and live below your means. Clothes in dumpsters and second hand stores aren't broke, but you could be if you don't look there.

Don't fall into the "NEW" trap. If certain brands of phones, cars, and other gadgets really need such high frequency revisions in the form of new releases, they should go out of business for constantly selling shitty products.

Don't fall into the "I can afford the monthly payment trap" on houses, cars, or other unnecessary shit.

Become the middleman.

8 hour work days are short when you own a business.

Don't buy stuff on credit unless it will make you more money than it costs, but you don't know if it will.

Many American businesses are set up to prey on weak minded people, especially credit card companies.

Credit can be caustic.

Leveraging high-risk investments is for losers, and lovers leave losers, so leveraging high-risk investments makes you lonely.

Some debts stick with you even after bankruptcy.

Investing = gambling. Anyone who tells you differently is probably trying to sell you something.

Invest only what you are willing to lose 100% of, even your credit score.

Investing time in the pursuit of knowledge has the highest return.

Do more than others to earn more than others.

Wealth Generating Assets go on sale too - remember the cost of housing during the Great Recession of 2008?

Don't let some perverted American dream consume you. Life doesn't need to be very costly if you have low bills.

The greed of the American consumer has fueled the socioeconomic gap through the pursuit of a fancy house, car, boat, and all the other money sucking bullshit, making the producers rich and the majority of consumers poor.

Even rich people can become poor when they become overly consumed with needing a pilot to fly their jet, a captain to sail their yacht, and storage to place these toys when not in use.

Greed knows no race, sex, religion, or bounds.

Money can be used to climb out of the wretched system, helping future generations be free from wage slavery and able to spend more time in the pursuit of family, knowledge, and things which matter most.

Road to Wealth

In Chapter 1 I said to think of wealth accumulation as a probability problem. We can now see a variety of events to pursue which will hopefully increase your chances of becoming and staying wealthy. Personally, my main motivator to accumulate wealth is bringing more freedom to myself and my family, and living a minimalist life allows me to do so without being a multi-millionaire. When you have enough money in the bank at any given time to pay 20 years of your kind of expenses - future inflation accounted for, or at least attempted - you have the opportunity to focus on what matters to you, and you don't have to work crazy hours just to pay the bills. What helps me maintain a positive attitude and work ethic is to focus on what I do have and not pour all of my attention into chasing the dollar. I am an advocate of trying to see the positive in every situation - you never know what positive situation a struggle will lead to, or help you overcome in the future - so don't wait for some certain amount of money to be happy; you'll probably never get happiness if so. If you think my mood and outlook is always positive, don't kid yourself, I'm human just like you and still struggle with anxiety, depression, and negative thoughts about money and everything else. Being positive and happy is something worth striving for though, and it's more fun than being depressed. Alright, enough preaching, here is a list of the main actionable advice from this book:

1. Analyze your spending, create a budget and stick to it. MINT and other similar software is very helpful with connecting your income and expenses and allowing you to stick to your budget and track those sneaky monthly subscription amounts.

   Actions:
   a. **Open a high yield bank account such as Wealthfront, and a high-yield checking account for your expenses.**
   b. Estimate your taxes for the year using a tax calculator, such as SmartAsset used in Chapter 2, so you know how much to save each month and how much net income you have to budget.
   c. **Open a budgeting account such as MINT and add your budget and hook up all accounts, credit cards, bills, etc...**

      d. Download an app to work on your credit, such as Credit Karma.

2. Become a person with sought after skills. Knowledge helps you to stand out from other job applicants. In addition to giving you a degree, college can also foster business ideas and networks. Learn as much as you can through College, MOOCS, and other affordable or free avenues.

    Actions:
      a. Talk to an adviser at a community college to find out what you can do today to get into a great career.
      b. Head to FAFSA and fill out their free form to see what you can qualify for.
      c. Sign up at Coursera, or some other free online course site to start learning new skills immediately.

3. Start to invest in your future, based on your budget. You can open retirement accounts through Wealthfront or similar online financial institutions.

    Action:
      a. Open a ROTH IRA to take advantage of tax-free compound interest accumulation, as well as an investment account. Add whatever amount your budget says to add to each account.

4. Understand the basics of taxes, where they go and how to lower them. Find and develop relationships with money management professionals: CPAs, Attorneys, Financial Advisors.

    Actions:
      a. Google Best CPA Financial Planner and contact one today.
      b. Start watching Clear Value Tax's YouTube channel.
      c. Check out Credit Karma Tax.

5. Step up your math game.
    Actions:
      a. Go through the investing math chapter and all of its exercises to beef up your general understanding of risk, investments and correlations.
      b. If you need help with math, sign up for a free account

with Khan Academy and start where you need. You can also find beginner to advanced math topics at Coursera.

6. Consider Minimalism.

   Actions to NOT DO:
   a. **Watch people on social media flaunt their love for living in a tent.**

Wealth generation is not usually fast or easy. It takes patience, discipline, ingenuity, and the desire to hustle. Although I went from having practically nothing to an insane amount of money (for me) within a 3 year time span, I truly believe I couldn't have done it without many of my previous experiences and close network of friends and family. I definitely would not be where I am today without the help of my pops Robert, my mom Rhonda, my brothers Austin and Dalton, and my best friend Adam who motivated me to go to college with him. Going through college gave me valuable math, research and programming education - prior to college, the only math education I had was from a failed pre-algebra course, so none - which in turn gave me business insights for many of the business problems I faced, and still face today. College also led me to meet my wife Tanya and have my awesome daughter Ellie. I hope the advice from this book helps you increase your wealth, in measures of both finance and happiness, by some relevant amount as implementing it has increased mine. Thank you for reading.

Take care!

Jordan Du Bois

Appendix

Links to Sites Found in Each Chapter & Other Helpful Links.
Scan the below QR code to be taken to a spreadsheet with all these links, if you are reading the paperback version:

Budget Basics:
Simple Tax Calculator Used for Each Scenario:
https://smartasset.com/taxes/income-taxes
Closing Credit Cards Properly:
https://www.experian.com/blogs/ask-experian/will-closing-a-credit-card-hurt-your-credit/
Government covered living expenses:
https://www.usa.gov/benefits
IRS Credits and Deductions
https://www.irs.gov/credits-deductions-for-individuals
Federal Wage:
https://www.dol.gov/general/topic/wages/minimumwage
Family Budget Calculator:
https://www.epi.org/resources/budget/
Inflation Adjusted Investment Calculator (ugly):
https://www.bankrate.com/calculators/retirement/roi-calculator.aspx
MINT Budgeting App:
https://www.mint.com/
Credit Karma App:
https://www.creditkarma.com/
Income Information:

https://www.census.gov/library/publications/2020/demo/p60-270.html#:~:text=Median%20household%20income%20was%20%2468%2C703,and%20Table%20A%2D1)

Spreadsheet Budget Video:
https://youtu.be/s8_mFmJ_e_o

Self-Directed IRA Custodians:
http://selfdirectedira.nuwireinvestor.com/list-of-self-directed-ira-custodians/

Types of Retirement Plans (IRS):
https://www.irs.gov/retirement-plans/plan-sponsor/types-of-retirement-plans

SoFi Automated Financial Planner:
https://www.sofi.com/no-cost-financial-planning/

Increase Value, Increase Pay:

FAFSA Application:
https://studentaid.gov/h/apply-for-aid/fafsa

Scholarships:
https://studentaid.gov/understand-aid/types/scholarships

529 College Plan:
https://www.sec.gov/reportspubs/investor-publications/investorpubsintro529htm.html#:~:text=A%20529%20plan%20is%20a,of%20the%20Internal%20Revenue%20Code.

Items covered by 529 Plan:
https://www.savingforcollege.com/article/using-your-529-plan-to-pay-for-room-and-board#:~:text=Room%20and%20board%20costs%20make,cost%20of%20a%20meal%20plan

College Scorecard:
https://collegescorecard.ed.gov/

Post Secondary Employment Outcomes:
https://lehd.ces.census.gov/data/pseo_explorer.html

Find Salary and Experience Info:
http://Salary.com
https://www.google.com/search?q=jobs+near+me

Coursera MOOCS:
https://www.coursera.org/

My Other Books:
http://www.ascendbiology.com/

ANKI Spaced Repetition Flashcards:
https://apps.ankiweb.net/

Hiring Test Creators:
https://vendordirectory.shrm.org/category/pre-employment-testing-screening?_ga=2.81904534.1801154963.1597670799-898454682.1597670799

Exploring PSEO Video:
https://youtu.be/YcW1ctdAANM

Taxes:
More on Lowering Taxes:
https://www.nolo.com/legal-encyclopedia/seven-steps-lower-taxes-29977.html
Tax Calculator with tax accounting explanations:
https://www.calculator.net/tax-calculator.html
Deductions VS Credits:
https://www.creditkarma.com/tax/i/tax-deduction-and-tax-credit
Plumber Salary:
https://money.usnews.com/careers/best-jobs/plumber/salary
Minimize Taxes Using Asset Location:
https://www.investopedia.com/articles/tax/08/asset-location.asp
LLC for Estate Planning:
https://www.investopedia.com/articles/personal-finance/071514/using-llc-estate-planning.asp
Tax Shelters:
https://www.investopedia.com/articles/personal-finance/032116/top-6-strategies-protect-your-income-taxes.asp
IRS Audit Info
IRS Audit Stats and IRS Audit News
Taxes and Rentals (Investopedia):
https://www.investopedia.com/articles/personal-finance/121415/how-prevent-tax-hit-when-selling-rental-property.asp
Credit Karma Tax:
https://www.creditkarma.com/tax
Congressional Budget Office:
https://www.cbo.gov/system/files/2019-11/55824-CBO-MBR-FY19.pdf
Total US Wages Earned Data:
https://fred.stlouisfed.org/series/BA06RC1A027NBEA
Center on Budget and Policy Priorities:
https://www.cbpp.org/research/

More Money Math:
Experian - How Does Credit Card Interest Work?
https://www.experian.com/blogs/ask-experian/how-does-credit-card-interest-work/#:~:text=Most%20credit%20card%20issuers%20will,next%20day's%20average%20daily%20balance
Investopedia - Simple VS Compound Interest:

https://www.investopedia.com/articles/investing/020614/learn-simple-and-compound-interest.asp

Financial Math and calculators:
http://www.moneychimp.com/

Consumer Price Index FAQs:
https://www.bls.gov/cpi/questions-and-answers.htm

Wealthfront Portfolio Performance:
https://www.wealthfront.com/historical-performance

Vanguard Total Stock Market Index Fund:
https://investor.vanguard.com/mutual-funds/profile/performance/vtsax

Vanguard Portfolio Allocation Models:
https://personal.vanguard.com/us/insights/saving-investing/model-portfolio-allocations

Laplace's Demon:
https://en.wikipedia.org/wiki/Laplace%27s_demon

Fat-Tailed Portfolio Creation Paper:
http://projects.nber.org/projects_backend/rrc/papers/orrc09-16.pdf

Stock Market Data:
http://www.crsp.org/

More Stock Market Data from Robert Shiller:
http://www.econ.yale.edu/~shiller/data.htm

Liquidity-based Portfolio Creation using Markov Chains:
http://www.paulorodrigues.pro.br/ojs/ijmp/index.php/ijmp/article/view/156/387

How Investing Can Kill You Video:
https://youtu.be/LGgewFSN110

Real Estate Investing Leverage Video:
https://youtu.be/1vbff7QUu9g

Finding Rental Investments Video:
https://youtu.be/3QvDPmh_x-0

World's Best Guys YouTube Channel:
https://www.youtube.com/channel/UC9Ui406nYyvBGkJAlaKe4ag?

Comparison of frequentist and Bayesian inference:
https://ocw.mit.edu/courses/mathematics/18-05-introduction-to-probability-and-statistics-spring-2014/readings/MIT18_05S14_Reading20.pdf

Top 10 US Economic Indicators:
https://www.investopedia.com/articles/personal-finance/020215/top-ten-us-economic-indicators.asp

ABOUT THE AUTHOR

Jordan DuBois is a stranger-than-fiction character. His life thus far has been that akin to a Blockbuster movie (think Good Will Hunting). Earning two Bachelor's degrees in arguably two of the most challenging fields, Applied Mathematics and Biology, coupled with his impoverished background and rough upbringing, Jordan has exceptional insight into how the financial aspects of living in America work. He has lived on the street, lived in a car, lived near, lived far. Quite frankly, he's been everywhere, man. Before hitting #RichBoy status with his tech and real estate companies - Reflecting Walls Photography, EasyPix, and Template Trainer, to name the largest contributors - Jordan was literally on food stamps and financial aid. His perspectives on life and the pursuit of dollar-derived happiness are like none other. Also, he wrote this bio, so take it with a grain of salt.

www.ingramcontent.com/pod-product-compliance
Lightning Source LLC
Chambersburg PA
CBHW040322220526
45473CB00009B/2536